Lecture Notes in Computer Science 13120

More information about this subseries at https://link.springer.com/bookseries/7411

Juan Moreno García-Loygorri ·
Antonio Pérez Yuste · Marion Berbineau (Eds.)

Communication Technologies for Vehicles

16th International Workshop
Nets4Cars/Nets4Trains/Nets4Aircraft 2021
Madrid, Spain, November 16–17, 2021
Revised Selected Papers

Springer

Editors
Juan Moreno García-Loygorri ⓘ
Technical University of Madrid
Madrid, Spain

Antonio Pérez Yuste ⓘ
Universidad Politécnica de Madrid
Madrid, Madrid, Spain

Marion Berbineau
Université Gustave Eiffel
Champs-sur-Marne, France

ISSN 0302-9743   ISSN 1611-3349 (electronic)
Lecture Notes in Computer Science
ISBN 978-3-030-92683-0   ISBN 978-3-030-92684-7 (eBook)
https://doi.org/10.1007/978-3-030-92684-7

LNCS Sublibrary: SL5 – Computer Communication Networks and Telecommunications

This Springer imprint is published by the registered company Springer Nature Switzerland AG
The registered company address is: Gewerbestrasse 11, 6330 Cham, Switzerland

Preface

The Communication Technologies for Vehicles Workshop series provides an international forum on the latest technologies and research in the field of intra- and inter-vehicles communications. This workshop is organized annually to present original research results in areas related to the physical layer, communication protocols and standards, mobility and traffic models, experimental and field operational testing, and performance analysis.

First launched by Tsutomu Tsuboi, Alexey Vinel, and Frei Liu in Saint Petersburg, Russia (2009), the Nets4Workshops series have been held in Newcastle upon Tyne, UK (2010), Oberpfaffenhofen, Germany (2011), Vilnius, Lithuania (2012), Villeneuve-d'Ascq, France (2013), Offenburg, Germany (spring 2014), Saint Petersburg, Russia (fall 2014), Sousse, Tunisia (2015), San Sebastián, Spain (2016), Toulouse, France (2017), Madrid, Spain (2018), Colmar, France (2019), Bordeaux (2020), and Madrid again in 2021. These proceedings gather the papers presented at the 16th edition of the workshop, which took place in Madrid, Spain, in November 2021. The workshop was supported by the Universidad Politécnica de Madrid and Rohde & Schwarz.

The call for papers resulted in eight submissions. Each of them was assigned to the international Technical Program Committee to be reviewed by at least two independent reviewers. The co-chairs of the four Technical Program Committees (Nets4Cars, Nets4Trains, Nets4Airplanes, and Nets4Spacecrafts) selected eight full papers for publication in these proceedings and presentation at the workshop, six of them for Nets4Cars and two for Nets4Trains.

This year the keynote speakers were as follows:

- Cesar Briso, "Wide Band Critical Communications for High Dynamic Vehicles," Technical University of Madrid (UPM), Spain
- Alexey Vinel, "Autonomous Vehicles: Communication and Cooperation," Halmstad University, Sweden
- Bernd Holfeld, "5GRAIL," Deutsche Bahn AG, Germany.
- Ke Guan, "Towards 6G: Paradigm of Realistic Terahertz Channel Modeling," Beijing Jiaotong University, China

The general co-chairs and the Technical Program Committee (TPC) co-chairs extend a sincere "thank you" to all the authors who submitted the results of their recent research as well as to all the members of the hard-working comprehensive Technical Program Committee that worked on the reviews.

November 2021

Juan Moreno García-Loygorri
Antonio Pérez Yuste
Marion Berbineau
Jaizki Mendizábal
José Soler
Cesar Briso Rodriguez

Organization

General Co-chairs

Marion Berbineau   Université Gustave Eiffel, France
Juan Moreno García-Loygorri   Technical University of Madrid (UPM), Spain
Antonio Pérez Yuste   Technical University of Madrid (UPM), Spain

TPC Co-chair (Nets4Cars)

Marion Berbineau   Université Gustave Eiffel, France

TPC Co-chairs (Nets4Trains)

Jaizki Mendizábal   Centre of Studies and Technical Investigations of
     Gipuz-koa (CEIT), Spain
Juan Moreno García-Loygorri   Technical University of Madrid (UPM), Spain
José Soler   Technical University of Denmark (DTU),
     Denmark

TPC Co-chair (Nets4Airplanes)

Cesar Briso Rodriguez   Technical University of Madrid (UPM), Spain

TPC Co-chair (Nets4Spacecrafts)

Antonio Pérez Yuste   Technical University of Madrid (UPM), Spain

Steering Committee

Marion Berbineau   Université Gustave Eiffel, France
Mohaned Kassab   University of Monastir, Tunisia
Juan Moreno García-Loygorri   Technical University of Madrid (UPM), Spain
Alain Pirovano   National School of Civil Aviation (ENAC), France
Alexey Vinel   Halmstad University, Sweden

Technical Program Committee

Hasnaâ Aniss	Université Gustave Eiffel, France
Hakim Badis	Université Gustave Eiffel, France
Marion Berbineau	Université Gustave Eiffel, France
Juliette Marais	Université Gustave Eiffel, France
Sassi Maaloul	Université Gustave Eiffel, France
Jaizki Mendizabal	University of Navarra, Spain
Juan Moreno García-Loygorri	Technical University of Madrid (UPM), Spain
Antonio Perez Yuste	Technical University of Madrid (UPM), Spain
Patrick Sondi	Université du Littoral Côte d'Opale, France
Jose Soler	Technical University of Denmark (DTU), Denmark

Hosting Institution

Universidad Politécnica de Madrid, ETSIS Telecommunication, Spain

Organizing Committee

María de los Ángeles López Fernández	Technical University of Madrid (UPM), Spain
Juan Moreno García-Loygorri	Technical University of Madrid (UPM), Spain
Antonio Perez Yuste	Technical University of Madrid (UPM), Spain
César Rodríguez Serrano	Technical University of Madrid (UPM), Spain
Jesús Sánchez García	Technical University of Madrid (UPM), Spain

Sponsoring Institution

Rohde & Schwarz, Spain

Abstract of Invited Talks

Wide Band Critical Communications for High Dynamic Vehicles

Cesar Briso Rodriguez

Departamento Ingeniería Audiovisual y Comunicaciones. ETSIST UPM, Madrid, Spain
cesar.briso@upm.es

Currently, the development of highly dynamic vehicles and transport systems such as unmanned aerial vehicles (UAVs) that perform low-level flights over city or trains in vacuum tubes (Hyperloop) that move at speeds greater than 400 Km/h demand broadband communications for control, signaling and payload. However, current systems such as 5G are not designed for these applications, so it is necessary to carefully model the propagation in these environments and optimize the operation of the network to allow these critical applications. The objective is to give an overview of the communications problems on this complex environments and the solutions that are being implemented.

Autonomous Vehicles: Communication and Cooperation

Alexey Vinel

Halmstad University, Halmstad, Sweden
alexey.vinel@hh.se

We will share some of our recent experiences on research of autonomous vehicles with a focus on inter-vehicular communications and respective cooperative driving functionalities. A few mathematical models, simulation-based studies and real-world demonstrators will be discussed. One of the cooperative autonomous driving concepts named platooning, which is an automatic following of wirelessly connected vehicles very closely behind each other, will be presented slightly deeper. We will demonstrate on a simple model how the safety of the platooning functionality can be assessed by coupling the quality of inter-vehicular radio communications to the likelihood of a rear-end collision.

5GRAIL

Marion Berbineau

Gustave Eiffel University, Bordeaux, France
marion.berbineau@univ-eiffel.fr

The Future Railway Mobile Communication System (FRMCS) will be the 5G worldwide standard for railway operational communications, conforming to European regulation as well as responding to the needs and obligations of rail organisations outside of Europe.

The work on functional & technical requirements, functional and system specification, standardisation in 3GPP as well as regarding harmonised spectrum solutions is currently led by UIC, in cooperation with the whole railway sector. A major challenge is the update by the European Railway Agency of the Technical Specification for Interoperability of Control Command and Signalling (CCS TSI) by the end of 2022 with a full description of FRMCS with respect to functionalities for interoperability.

Therefore, the main objective of 5GRAIL is to validate the first set of FRMCS specifications (also called FRMCS V1) by developing and testing prototypes of the FRMCS ecosystem, for both trackside infrastructure and on-board.

The validation of the latest available railway-relevant 5G specification will be achieved through emulation of cross-border trials covering significant portions of railway operational communication requirements and including the core technological innovations for rail expected from 5G release 16 and pre-release 17.

The project will first define the functional tests and then work towards prototypes development and evaluation, for both on-board and infrastructure. Prototypes will be then tested in simulated and real environments, with pilots in labs and in the field rolled out in various European sites, in order to ensure compliances and validation for specification, standards and performance, and consequently guarantee the time to market for FRMCS products, planned for 2025 as per European timeline.

The project will finally deliver test report conclusions to update FRMCS V1 specification where needed and to identify technical constraints related to implementation issues.

5GRAIL outcomes are viewed by the railway sector as a key milestone in the global plan leading to FRMCS market readiness for railways in Europe.

Towards 6G: Paradigm of Realistic Terahertz Channel Modeling

Ke Guan

Beijing Jiaotong University, Beijing, China
k.guan@bjtu.edu.cn

Terahertz (THz) communications are envisioned as a key technology for the sixth-generation wireless communication system (6G). However, it is not practical to perform large-scale channel measurements with high degrees of freedom at THz frequency band. This makes empirical or stochastic modeling approaches relying on measurements no longer stand. In order to break through the bottleneck of scarce full-dimensional channel sounding measurements, this talk presents a novel paradigm for THz channel modeling towards 6G. With the core of high-performance ray tracing (RT), the presented paradigm requires merely quite limited channel sounding to calibrate the geometry and material electromagnetic (EM) properties of the three-dimensional (3D) environment model in the target scenarios. Then, through extensive RT simulations, the parameters extracted from RT simulations can be fed into either ray-based novel stochastic channel models or cluster-based standard channel model families. Verified by RT simulations, these models can generate realistic channels that are valuable for the design and evaluation of THz systems. Representing two ends of 6G THz use cases from microscopy to macroscopy, case studies are made for close-proximity communications, wireless connections on a desktop, and smart rail mobility, respectively. Last but not least, new concerns on channel modeling resulting from distinguishing features of THz wave are discussed regarding propagation, antenna array, and device aspects, respectively.

Contents

Nets4Cars

On the Performance of Inter User Coordination for Resource Allocation Enhancement in NR V2X Mode 2

Mohamed Shehata, Cristina Ciochina, and Jean-Christophe Sibel(✉)

Mitsubishi Electric R&D Centre Europe, Rennes, France
{c.ciochina,j.sibel}@fr.merce.mee.com

Abstract. The fifth generation (5G) new radio (NR) vehicle to everything (V2X) evolved as a key enabler in order to support advanced use cases for connected vehicles and automated driving applications with stringent reliability and latency requirements. One of the most significant parts of 5G NR V2X is the sidelink distributed resource allocation mode known as mode 2 in which vehicles do the resource allocation autonomously. This paper targets the third generation partnership (3GPP) 5G NR V2X mode 2 resource allocation enhancements, with a particular focus on inter user coordination between vehicles. Inter user coordination feature allows vehicles using the NR V2X mode 2 to exchange cooperation messages. Thus, acquiring additional information for resource allocation compared to the baseline fully distributed approach adopted in release 16, by overcoming the hidden node problem for instance. In this paper, we propose a practical inter user coordination framework for NR V2X mode 2 enhancement in different cast scenarios. Moreover, we show the gain achieved in packet reception ratio (PRR) by such framework using system level simulations.

Keywords: 5G · New radio (NR) · Vehicle to everything (V2X) · Resource allocation · Inter user coordination · Hidden node problem

1 Introduction

Advanced vehicle to everything (V2X) applications have recently emerged in order to support connected vehicles and fully autonomous vehicle scenarios. Such scenarios aim at enhancing the road safety, the driving experience and the traffic flow. However, such advanced V2X applications require ultra reliable low latency communication (URLLC) schemes which are hardly achievable by the current communication technologies.

The long term evolution (LTE) cellular V2X (C-V2X) was proposed by the third generation partnership project (3GPP) to address the basic safety applications for V2X. However, C-V2X fails to satisfy the stringent reliability and latency requirements imposed by advanced V2X applications [1]. NR V2X evolved in order to extend the achievable reliability and latency of C-V2X starting by release 16 [2].

© Springer Nature Switzerland AG 2021
J. Moreno García-Loygorri et al. (Eds.): Nets4Cars/Nets4Trains/Nets4Aircraft 2021, LNCS 13120, pp. 3–14, 2021.
https://doi.org/10.1007/978-3-030-92684-7_1

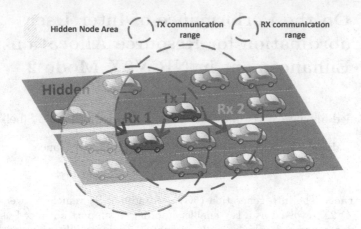

Fig. 1. Illustration of the hidden node problem in a typical V2X scenario.

In NR V2X, many new features are added compared to C-V2X such as flexible numerologies for subcarrier spacing (SCS) or advanced multiple access techniques [3]. Thus, the NR V2X uses such features to enhance the sidelink communication over the PC5 interface for basic safety applications [4] and also for advanced V2X applications [5].

In NR V2X two resource allocation modes exist, namely mode 1 and mode 2. In mode 1 the network infrastructure (eNodeB) overtakes the scheduling task of the sidelink resources for each vehicle within its coverage. In mode 2, each vehicle user equipment (UE) autonomously allocates its resources without any help from the network infrastructure. Thus, the resource allocation in mode 2 is based only on the vehicle UE's local sensing information, wherein the UE allocates a resource which is sensed as idle or with low level of interference [2].

In NR V2X release 17, one of the main objectives is to enhance sidelink transmissions and more specifically to enhance the resource allocation in the distributed mode 2. Inter-UE coordination was proposed as a promising feature for mode 2 resource allocation enhancement [6]. In NR release 16 some early studies were proposed to support inter-UE coordination as a sub mode for mode 2 referred to as mode 2 (b) [7], however, it did not enter the standardization phase. With the inter-UE coordination feature, a UE can send assisting information/reports to other UE(s) to help in their resource selection procedure. Thus, inter-UE coordination relaxes the fully distributed nature of NR V2X mode 2 by allowing for additional assistance information from other UE(s). Consequently the assisting report sent by the assisting UE can encompass some recommendations for the UE(s) receiving the assistance on whether to select or ignore a given resource in the resource allocation process. The contents of such assistance report are currently under discussion in 3GPP.

One of the main benefits of inter-UE coordination is to reduce the hidden node problem as shown in Fig. 1. In this example, the transmitter (Tx) UE (blue vehicle) is not aware of the hidden node (red vehicle) since it is outside its

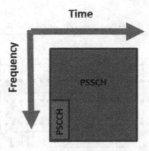

Fig. 2. PSCCH and PSSCH channels multiplexing.

communication range. Therefore, in case release 16 NR V2X mode 2 is applied, autonomous resource selection will be done based on local sensing at the Tx. In this case, the Tx can choose the same resource used by the hidden node as it is seen as idle resource based on its own sensing and thereafter causing a collision at the receiver (Rx) UE (red vehicle) which lies in the coverage of both the Tx and the hidden node. Assuming the inter-UE coordination feature is applied, the Rx UE can send an assistance report to the Tx UE informing it about the resource used by the hidden node, avoiding the collision that can result from the hidden node problem.

In this paper we introduce a realistic framework to apply inter-UE coordination for NR V2X in different cast transmissions. We evaluate the achievable packet reception ratio (PRR) of the proposed framework by system level simulations and compare it to the baseline release 16 NR V2X mode 2 in order to assess the benefits that can be achieved using our proposed inter-UE coordination framework.

2 3GPP NR V2X Mode 2

2.1 Physical Channels Multiplexing in NR Sidelink

Considering resource allocation for V2X for data and control transmissions, both physical sidelink control channel (PSCCH) and physical sidelink shared channel (PSSCH) are considered to form a resource pool to be shared between the vehicles. The PSSCH carries the transport block for data transmission, while PSCCH carries the sidelink control information (SCI) for control overhead transmission. In NR V2X PSSCH and PSCCH are multiplexed in both time and frequency as follows: part of PSCCH and the associated PSSCH are transmitted using overlapping time resources in non-overlapping frequency resources, but another part of the associated PSSCH and/or another part of the PSCCH are transmitted using non-overlapping time resources [8] as shown in Fig. 2.

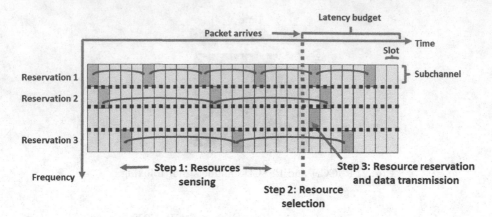

Fig. 3. Illustration of the three steps of resource allocation in 3GPP NR V2X mode 2

2.2 3GPP NR V2X Mode 2 Resource Pool

In NR PC5 sidelink, the time granularity for a resource is a slot. A slot consists of 14 OFDM symbols whose duration depends on the SCS in frequency. On the other hand, the frequency granularity for a resource is a subchannel consisting of at least 10 resource blocks (RBs), wherein a RB consists of 12 subcariers.

2.3 Resource Allocation for NR V2X Mode 2

The mode 2 resource reservation scheme is based on three consecutive steps [9] illustrated in Fig. 3 as follows:

– Step 1: Resource sensing
  A user attempts to find available time-frequency resource (subchannel(s)-slot resource) for its desired transmission. To know whether a resource is used or not by other users, the user tries to decode the SCI that is carried in the PSCCH to extract the resource reservation information, and after that the reference signal received power (RSRP) related to this SCI is measured. By the end of this step, the transmitter has a full map of the reserved resources and the free ones in the resource grid for a given sensing window size (1 s in LTE, flexible in NR) as shown in Fig. 3.
– Step 2: Resource selection
  The user randomly selects resources to use for its own transmission among all the resources in the candidate set, composed of the resources determined as free at the previous step.
– Step 3: Resource reservation and data transmission
  After the resource selection step, the transmitter assigns the data packet to a TB and transmits it in the PSSCH part of the selected resource as shown in Fig. 1. It also transmits the PSCCH containing the SCI related to the TB, which carries the resource reservation information as shown in Fig. 3.

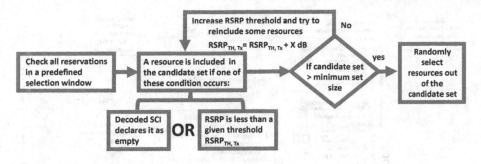

Fig. 4. Flowchart of the release 16 NR V2X mode 2 resource allocation.

3 Proposed Framework for Inter User Coordination

In order to clarify the difference between our proposed framework and the current baseline release 16 NR V2X mode 2 explained in the previous section, we summarize the baseline framework in the flowchart in Fig. 4. Thus, in this section we will clarify the mechanism of our proposed inter-UE framework for unicast and groupcast in comparison to the baseline scenario.

3.1 Inter User Coordination for Unicast Transmissions

In the unicast scenario, only one Rx UE exists and thus it can directly act as an assisting UE in which we refer to as UE-A. Similarly the Tx will be the UE that will receive the assistance report in order to consider it for its resource allocation procedure and we will refer to it as UE-B. Then, in this proposed framework UE-A will share its sensing information with UE-B. For instance, UE-A sends UE-B a report with all resources seen as busy from its sensing procedure and thus UE-B can exclude them from its candidate resources before resource selection, consequently avoiding the hidden node problem. However, in case the assistance report sent by UE-A cause an exhaustive exclusion of resources at UE-B side ending up with low amount of candidate resources for selection, UE-B will increase the RSRP threshold for resource exclusion at its side and this may reinclude some or all of the excluded resources by UE-A and thus retriggering the hidden node problem again by overriding the assistance information. In order to overcome such challenge imposed by the NR V2X mode 2 standard, we propose to prioritize/order the non preferred resources, based on their received RSRP value at UE-A side, in the assistance report sent by UE-A. In this way, when UE-B needs to re-include some of these non preferred resources it can follow an order starting from the least interfered resource to UE-A. The summary of this framework is given in Fig. 5.

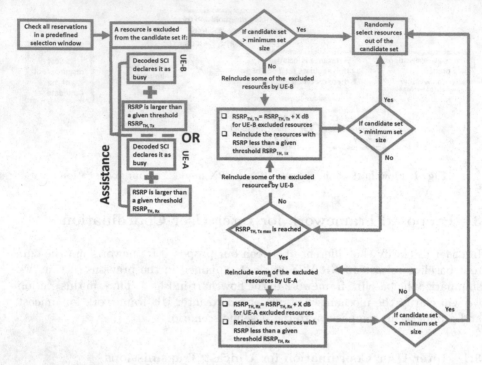

Fig. 5. Flowchart of the proposed inter-UE coordination for NR V2X mode 2 resource allocation.

3.2 Inter User Coordination for Groupcast/Broadcast Transmissions

In the Groupcast/Broadcast scenario, many Rx UEs exist. If all of the Rx UEs act as an assisting UE (UE-A), as shown in Fig. 6-a, the overhead would be excessive. It is clear that carefully selecting which UE(s) need to provide assistance is necessary for overhead mitigation. We propose a novel mechanism to determine which UE(s) in groupcast/broadcast transmission can act as UE-A and send assistance report to the Tx (UE-B). As shown in Fig. 6-b can relay most of the additional assistance information for UE-B compared to the case where all Rxs act as assisting UEs (UE-As) as shown in Fig. 6-a.

As shown in Fig. 6-b, the UEs in the outer part of the communication range of the Tx can cover approximately all the hidden nodes and expose them to the Tx (UE-B) through assistance information. Therefore, we propose in our framework that for a UE to act as UE-A, it needs to be geographically situated in the outer communication range of UE-B. That is explained as the distance d between that given UE and UE-B is bounded as follows $d_{min} < d < d_{max}$ where d_{min} and d_{max} are some preconfigured values that define the limits of the outer communication ring as shown in Fig. 7.

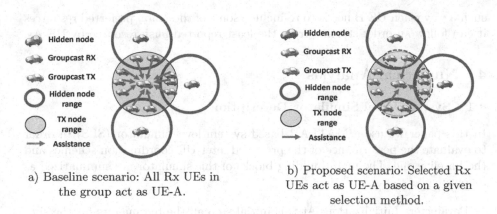

a) Baseline scenario: All Rx UEs in the group act as UE-A.

b) Proposed scenario: Selected Rx UEs act as UE-A based on a given selection method.

Fig. 6. Determining UE-A scenarios in groupcast transmissions

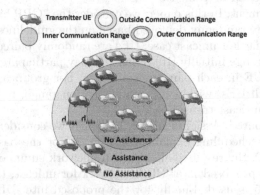

Fig. 7. Illustration of the selection mechanism for the assisting UEs (UE-As) in groupcast transmissions.

The UEs selected as assisting UEs (UE-As) can proceed with sending assistance reports including their non preferred resources similar to the unicast case summarized in Fig. 5. In case the assistance reports sent by UE-As cause an exhaustive exclusion of resources at UE-B side ending up with low amount of candidate resources for selection, UE-B will increase the RSRP threshold for resource exclusion at its side and this may reinclude some or all of the excluded resources by UE-As and thus re-triggering the hidden node problem again by overriding the assistance information. In order to overcome such challenge imposed by the NR V2X mode 2 standard, we propose to prioritize/order the non preferred resources, but this time using a different approach compared to the unicast case. We propose to prioritize the non preferred resources based on their number of occurrences in the assistance reports sent by UE-As.

For example a resource being reported as busy by 3 UE-As has higher priority to be excluded compared to a resource being reported as busy by one UE-A. In such a way when UE-B needs to re-include some of these non preferred resources it can follow an order starting from the least reported busy resource by UE-As.

4   Numerical Analysis

4.1   System Level Simulator Description

In this paper we use a MATLAB based system level simulator (SLS) in order to evaluate the performance of the proposed inter-UE coordination schemes and the baseline one. The main building blocks of this simulator are summarized as follows:

- Parameters Initialization: At this initial step all the parameters for the simulation scenario are defined. A summary for the simulation parameters used in this paper is given in Table 1.
- Vehicles' Deployment: In this paper, we consider the 3GPP highway scenario, where vehicles are randomly deployed based on the guidelines defined in [10].
- Users' Assignment: For unicast case: UEs are randomly paired, within the Tx communication range initially [10]. Each UE may participate only in a single pair. Only one UE in each pair transmit data. For groupcast case: A given Tx UE selects all UEs, within its communication range, to be receivers for its groupcast/multicast transmissions [10].
- First Radio Resources Assignment: In this paper we consider periodic traffic with SPS-based scheduling explained in Sect. 2. For the baseline release 16 NR V2X mode 2, the resource allocation framework summarized in Fig. 4 is applied. For the proposed inter-UE framework for unicast, the scheme summarized in Fig. 5 is used. Finally for the proposed inter-UE framework for groupcast/multicast, the UE-As selection scheme described in Fig. 7 is applied together with the scheme summarized in Fig. 5.
- Position Update: With the simulation time, given the mobility of the UEs, their positions are updated every 1 ms.
- Quality Assessment: With the simulation time, given the mobility of the UEs, all the simulation variables dependant on the positions of the UEs are updated each 1 ms such as the pathloss, SNR, SINR, etc.
- Radio Resources Reassignment: With the simulation time, each UE that needs to make a new reservation due to the expiry of its current reservation of a given resource will relaunch a resource allocation procedure similar to the one explained in the 'First Radio Resources Assignment' bullet point.
- Performance evaluation: Finally after the end of the simulation time, the PRR is calculated versus distance for each simulated scheme. The PRR at a given Tx-Rx distance d is calculated as follows:

$$PRR(d) = \frac{\text{no. of correctly decoded packets (d)}}{\text{no. of transmitted packets (d)}} \qquad (1)$$

4.2   Performance Evaluation

In Fig. 8, the PRR gain that can be achieved using our proposed unicast inter-UE coordination framework over the baseline release 16 NR V2X mode 2 is highlighted. Figure 8 considers a scenario with periodic traffic, wherein the Tx has knowledge of the busy resources determined by the Rx sensing information in case the proposed inter-UE coordination is applied. The simulations parameters are summarized in Table 1, while the unicast inter-UE coordination framework applied is described in Subsect. 3-A and summarized in Fig. 5. In the simulated scenario, the Tx communication range is ≈420 m. The PRR gain of the proposed inter-UE coordination framework over the baseline release 16 NR V2X mode 2 in the simulated scenario is up to ≈10%. This PRR gain increases with distance within the Tx communication range, then this PRR gain starts to diminish at higher distances since the communication becomes noise limited rather than interference limited. Thus, when the Tx-Rx distance surpasses the Tx communication range, both schemes are mainly limited by the high propagation pathloss. Therefore, it can be concluded that the PRR gain achieved by the proposed inter-UE coordination over the baseline NR V2X mode 2 arises from the elimination of the hidden node problem in the interference limited scenarios (wherein the hidden node interference is the dominant loss compared to the propagation pathloss).

In Fig. 9 the PRR gain that can be achieved using our proposed groupcast/multicast inter-UE coordination framework over the baseline release 16 NR V2X mode 2 is highlighted. Figure 9 considers a scenario with periodic traffic, wherein the Tx has knowledge of the busy resources determined by a given set of the groupcast Rxs' sensing information, in case the proposed inter-UE coordination is applied. The simulations parameters are summarized in Table 1, while the groupcast/multicast inter-UE coordination framework applied is described in Subsect. 3-B and summarized in Figs. 5, 6 and 7. In the simulated scenario, the Tx communication range is ≈420 m. The Rx UEs of the groupcast are updated each 1 s, in order to ensure that only UEs within the Tx communication range are considered as Rx UEs. Based on our proposed inter-UE coordination framework, only a set of selected UEs in the groupcast provide assistance to the Tx (i.e. only a set of selected UEs act as UE-As).

The set of selected UEs to provide assistance (UE-As) in case the proposed inter-UE coordination framework is applied ensures that such vehicles are bounded in a ring with lower limit d_{min} and upper limit d_{max} as shown in Fig. 7. In Fig. 9 we consider some options of d_{min} and d_{max} as follows:

- Assistance ($d_{min} = 0$, $d_{max} = 1.1$)× Comm. range: All UEs with Tx-Rx distance d in the range 0 m $< d <$ (1.1 × Comm. range) m are selected as UE-As and thus, sending assistance to the Tx UE (UE-B).
- Assistance ($d_{min} = 0.5$, $d_{max} = 1.1$)× Comm. range: All UEs with Tx-Rx distance d in the range (0.5 × Comm. range) m $< d <$ (1.1 × Comm. range) m are selected as UE-As and thus, sending assistance to the Tx UE (UE-B).

– Assistance ($d_{min} = 0.9$, $d_{max} = 1.1$)× Comm. range: All UEs with Tx-Rx distance d in the range $(0.9 \times$ Comm. range$)$ m $< d < (1.1 \times$ Comm. range$)$ m are selected as UE-As and thus, sending assistance to the Tx UE (UE-B).

The upper limit for UE-A selection d_{max} is set to $d_{max} = 1.1 \times$ communication range in order to consider the vehicles' displacement in the 1 s time interval between each groupcast formation update. The vehicles' displacement in that 1 s is ≈10% of the used communication range in the simulated scenario.

In the simulated scenario in Fig. 9, the total number of UEs dropped in the highway scenario defined in Table 1 is 168 UEs. Out of these UEs, ≈35 UEs on average are within the Tx communication range (i.e. groupcast Rxs) at a given time instant. In option ($d_{min} = 0.5$, $d_{max} = 1.1$)× Comm. range, ≈18.5 UEs on average are within the specified ring, thus acting as UE-A and delivering assistance to the Tx UE (UE-B). While in option ($d_{min} = 0.9$, $d_{max} = 1.1$)× Comm. range, ≈3.5 UEs on average are within the specified ring, thus acting as UE-A and delivering assistance to the Tx UE (UE-B).

Moreover, in the simulated highway scenario defined in Table 1, d_{min} is clearly higher than the road width ($d_{min} > 24$ m). Thus, choosing UEs in the outer ring of the Tx communication range is equivalent to choosing some front and rear vehicles between d_{min} and d_{max} from the Tx, in this proposed highway scenario. Taking this into consideration, together with the fact that nearby UEs exhibit approximately similar sensing information as shown in Fig. 6, we propose two more options for UE-As selection as follows:

– 2 UEs (1 front - 1 back): In this option only 1 UE at the front of the Tx UE is randomly selected from the range $(d_{min}, d_{max}) = (0.5, 1.1)$ to act as a front UE-A. Similarly, only 1 UE at the back of the Tx UE is randomly selected from the range $(d_{min}, d_{max}) = (0.5, 1.1)$ to act as a back UE-A.
– 4 UEs (2 front - 2 back): In this option, only 2 UEs at the front of the Tx UE are randomly selected from the ranges $(d_{min}, d_{max}) = (0.5, 0.75)$ and $(d_{min}, d_{max}) = (0.75, 1.1)$ respectively to act as front UE-As. Similarly, only 2 UEs at the back of the Tx UE are randomly selected from the ranges $(d_{min}, d_{max}) = (0.5, 0.75)$ and $(d_{min}, d_{max}) = (0.75, 1.1)$ respectively to act as back UE-As.

The results in Fig. 9 show that the PRR gain of the proposed groupcast inter-UE coordination framework over the baseline release 16 NR V2X mode 2 in the simulated scenario is up to ≈7% when all UEs in the Tx communication range act as UE-As and send assistance reports. However, this can be overhead consuming from the network point of view as previously mentioned. Thus, in Fig. 9, the PRR results of the proposed distance based UE-As selection methods are presented. It is shown that using such distance based UE-As selection options, significant PRR gain can still be achieved over the baseline release 16 NR V2X mode 2 resource allocation, with minimal additional overhead requirement. For example, it is clarified in Fig. 9 that selecting only 4 UEs to act as UE-As (in a well distributed manner) can achieve approximately the same PRR gain achieved by the case when all UEs in Tx communication range act as UE-As.

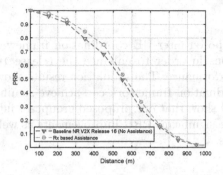

Fig. 8. PRR comparison between the baseline release 16 NR V2X mode 2 and the proposed inter-UE coordination enhancement framework for unicast transmissions.

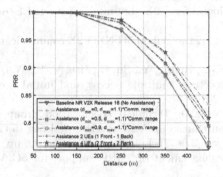

Fig. 9. PRR comparison between the baseline release 16 NR V2X mode 2 and the proposed inter-UE coordination enhancement framework for groupcast transmissions.

Table 1. Simulation parameters

Parameter	Value
Deployment scenario	Highway Option A scenario [10]
	Road length = 4 km
	Number of lanes = 6 (3 in each direction)
	Vehicle speed = 140 km/h
	Vehicle density = 7 vehicles/km/lane
Channel model	NR V2X channel model [10]
Carrier frequency, SCS	6 GHz, 15 KHz
Simulated bandwidth	20 MHz
Tx power	23 dBm
Tx & Rx antenna gain	3 dB
Inter-packet arrival time	20 ms
Selection window size	20 ms
Payload, MCS	400 Byte, 16-QAM, LDPC (CR = 0.5)

5   Conclusion

In this paper, we proposed inter-UE coordination frameworks for unicast and groupcast transmissions in order to enhance the release 16 NR V2X mode 2 resource allocation performance. The simulation results show that our proposed unicast inter-UE coordination framework can achieve significant PRR improvements. Moreover, they show that our proposed groupcast inter-UE coordination framework can achieve significant PRR improvements as well, even with limited overhead requirements.

References

1. Naik, G., Choudhury, B., Park, J.-M.: IEEE 802.11bd 5G NR V2X: evolution of radio access technologies for V2X communications. IEEE Access **7**, 70169–70184 (2019)
2. Garcia, M.H.C., et al.: A tutorial on 5G NR V2X communications. IEEE Commun. Surv. Tutorials 1 (2021)
3. Lien, S.-Y., Shieh, S.-L., Huang, Y., Su, B., Hsu, Y.-L., Wei, H.-Y.: 5G new radio: waveform, frame structure, multiple access, and initial access. IEEE Commun. Mag. **55**(6), 64–71 (2017)
4. 3GPP TR 22.185 v15.0.0: Technical specification group services and system aspects: Service requirements for V2X services. Release 15 (2018)
5. 3GPP TR 22.886 v16.2.0: Technical specification group services and system aspects. Study on enhancement of 3GPP support for 5G V2X services. Release 15 (2018)
6. LG Electronics: RP-193257. New WID on NR sidelink enhancement. 3GPP TSG RAN Meeting 86, Sitges, Spain (2019)
7. LG Electronics: R1-1912588. Discussion on resource allocation for Mode 2. 3GPP TSG RAN WG1 Meeting 99, Reno, USA (2019)
8. 3GPP TR 37.985 V1.1.0: Overall description of RAN aspects for Vehicle-to-everything (V2X) based on LTE and NR. Release 16 (2020)
9. 3GPP TR 38.885 V2.0.0: Study on NR Vehicle-to-Everything (V2X) (2019)
10. 3GPP TR 37.885 V1.0.0: Study on evaluation methodology of new Vehicle-to Everything (V2X) use cases for LTE and NR (2018)

Operational Deployment of GNSS Anti-spoofing System for Road Vehicles

Francisco Gallardo López[1](✉) ⓘ and Antonio Pérez Yuste[2] ⓘ

[1] DLR GfR MbH, Universidad Politécnica de Madrid, Madrid, Spain
francisco.gallardo@dlr-gfr.com
[2] Communications and A/V Engineering, Universidad Politécnica de Madrid, Madrid, Spain
antonio.perez@upm.es

Abstract. This paper presents the design and operational implementation of a GNSS anti-spoofing system, and provides a first set results with real signals. The work discussed here is based on a validated proof of concept of a SCER (Secure Code Estimation and Replay) spoofing detector, and represents a first operational prototype towards the development of a global GNSS anti-spoofing network. Both the proof of concept and the prototype are based on Machine Learning (ML) techniques and novel signal features extraction. Its future usage in road transportation environments is discussed.

Keywords: Cybersecurity · Galileo · GNSS authentication · GNSS security · Machine learning · SCER · Road transportation

1 Introduction

Global Navigation Satellite Systems (GNSS) dependant services are potentially vulnerable to the reception and usage of false GNSS signals that may be injected into the victim's receiver on purpose, or not. Attacks based on generating fake GNSS signals to gain an illegitimate advantage are known as Spoofing attacks.

Spoofing attacks are a very serious threat for any GNSS based system in time synchronization and/or positioning services. The victim might obtain a false clock offset, a false position fix, of both. As a consequence, for example, any autonomous vehicle could be steered off course with very serious consequences. This paper will discuss the first steps made by the authors towards the practical implementation of the spoofing detection system proposed in [1] in the road vehicles market. In the context of autonomous operations, such a risk needs to be considered and reliable and real time detection methodologies are required.

This work was possible due to the agreement between DLR GfR mbH and the Technical University of Madrid for the development of an industrial PhD for researching SCER OS-NMA anti-spoofing protection techniques.

Numerous examples of past GNSS Spoofing attacks in the mobility context are reported in the literature.

This paper discusses a practical implementation of an operational system based on Machine Learning (ML) for protecting GNSS receivers, in a road transportation environment, from GNSS Spoofing attacks. The work presented here provides the results in terms of performance of the operational system prototype developed by the authors.

This paper is divided into the following 6 sections: Sect. 1 introduces this paper and briefly describes the signal features extraction and Machine Learning (ML) algorithms proposed in [1]. Section 2 outlines the development of the operational system implemented. Section 4 explains the testing methodology of the system with real signals. In Sect. 5, the results are provided. Finally, in Sect. 6, the conclusions are outlined.

1.1 Machine Learning Techniques for SCER Spoofing Attacks Detection

Authors in [1] proposed a novel theoretical approach to extract a set of GNSS signal features to be fed into Machine Learning (ML) algorithms in order to detect GNSS Spoofing attacks. The paper was mainly focused on detecting Secure Code Estimation and Replay (SCER) spoofing attacks, as these may still be a serious challenge even for future GNSS protection systems like Navigation Message Authentication (NMA) [2] or Spreading Code Authentication (SCA) [3]. SCER spoofing attacks consists on receiving the positioning signal from real navigation satellites, decoding the navigation message, and synthesizing a new signal with a fake navigation message able to mislead a GNSS receiver. Nonetheless, the described protection techniques can also be applied to other types of Spoofing attacks, as long as open-sky conditions are met and the Spoofer is not able to tamper with the victim's receiver antenna. Such assumption holds particularly well for GNSS receivers in Critical Infrastructure systems, but could be problematic in road transportation use cases. As it will be discussed in Sect. 3, tailoring of the system for such environment is needed.

The complementary (to the Galileo Navigation Message Authentication) detection method for end-user receivers against spoofing attacks, proposed in [1], extracts a set of features from the receiver's search space for each specific satellite, including Radio Frequency Interference (RFI) detection in the time domain.

Then, by properly training an ML algorithm, such as: Decision Trees, ADABoost (Adaptating Boosting) or Random Forest, the presence of any attacker could be easily detected. The main process is therefore divided into two main steps: the features extraction step and the ML detection stage.

These two steps are the classical steps in any Machine Learning (ML) problem, where first the problem and the usable features are extracted and then the most adequate model configuration is found [4].

1.2   Features Extraction

One of the contributions presented in [1] was the extraction process to obtain a set of signal features from the GNSS search space. This set is determined by the next two processes: the Model-Gaussian Signal (MGS) extraction and the radio interference (RFI) detection.

- **MGS extraction:** It consists of an iterative process of 2D Gaussian fitting in a time-frequency domain, and a further process to extract the main features of the received signal. The remaining noise baseline, after the extraction, is also estimated.
- **RFI detection:** It performs a parallel search in the time domain for RFI signals, so it ensures that, should an attack starts by blinding the victim's receiver, it can be detected and flagged.

1.3   Machine Learning Detection

Based on the calculated features, ML algorithms are applied, as described in [1]. The best algorithms, in terms of PFA (Probability of False Alarm) and PMD (Probability of Missed Detection), were those based on Decision Trees, Random Forest and ADA Boost.

The selected Machine Learning algorithms were picked among others non-decision tress based (e.g. Neural Network). The selection of such algorithms was performed based on the work in [1]. These algorithms demonstrated a better F1 score, which is a figure of merit commonly used to evaluate the performance of machine learning and data mining algorithms. F1 score takes both false positives and false negatives into account and synthesizes quite well how precise and sensitive the algorithm is [4].

The configuration for the algorithms (in all the reported results) was the same ones that were reported in such article, namely:

1. Decision Tree: Max depth = 7, Minimum number of samples per split = 3.
2. Random Forest: Max depth = 7, Minimum number of samples per split = 3, Number of trees in the random forest = 10.
3. AdaBoost: Number of estimators = 50.

2   Practical Implementation of the Protection System

In [1], a proof of concept for a SCER spoofing detector was validated by using simulated data. Based on the work developed for this purpose, the contribution of this paper is focused on the development of a system to put the proposed algorithm to a test. Based on that, the results of the operational system that could detect the Spoofing attack in the received signals *in real time* and the results of the testing with real signals are provided.

2.1   Overall Architecture

In Fig. 1, the upgrades to the Workbench for GNSS Spoofing testing, with respect to those presented in [1], can be seen. The adaptation of interfaces to allow testing (where the signal is fed via network UDP sockets) of the real time receiver system was performed, and is presented for the first time here. This implied creating casters and file readers to play back recorded signals (Spoofed or not), as well as the development of the necessary software (SW) to allow the feeding RT (Real Time) signals (directly from the front-end) to the receiver under test. The SW was ported to Docker to allow a better development and deployment process and an improved operational system configuration control. The usage of containers provides better modularity and scalability, as supporting more remote front-ends is performed by deploying more containers.

The system relies on distributed SDR (Software Defined Radio) digitizers that send the signal to the Central ML Computation Unit (CMCU) via a secure and private network. Then, the CMCU algorithm determines whether the signal is spoofing-free or not. The CMCU system is deployed inside of the so-called, "GNSS Receiver protected with ML" subsystem in Fig. 1, as the Workbench allows the test of different protection methods, not only those based on ML.

The CMCU in the Operational deployment can be seen in Fig. 2. This pseudo-real time SW, developed in Python, takes advantage of the multiprocessing capabilities of Python by means of making extensive usage of the "Multiprocessing" library.

Once it is launched (via a pre-configured Docker image), the orchestrator reads the configuration of the protection system, among others. It includes the number of channels, the IP and ports of the front-ends, logging level, product archive location, etc. At the Operating System (OS) level, it also launches a process per receiving channel, and one extra process ("Signal Consumer") per front-end. That way, by means of queues, the Signal consumer tackles the reception via a UDP socket of samples from one front-end (per port), and then distributes the samples to each channel.

All SW parts (orchestrator, signal consumer and each one of the channels) run in different processes, allowing us to take advantage of the multi-core structure of modern computers, which is key for its proper real time performance.

The orchestractor then collects the reports for each period from all channels available, providing the operator with the information regarding the ML assessment per channel (per satellite).

The operational system is able to provide one spoofing assessment every 400 ms (average value). This result is obtained by running the Operational deployment in docker image on a standard laptop with 8 vCPUs (Intel Core i7-10510U CPU@1.8 GHz) and 32 GB of RAM. Only one channel was configured for the speed test. The global performance could be increased when launched in a dedicated server.

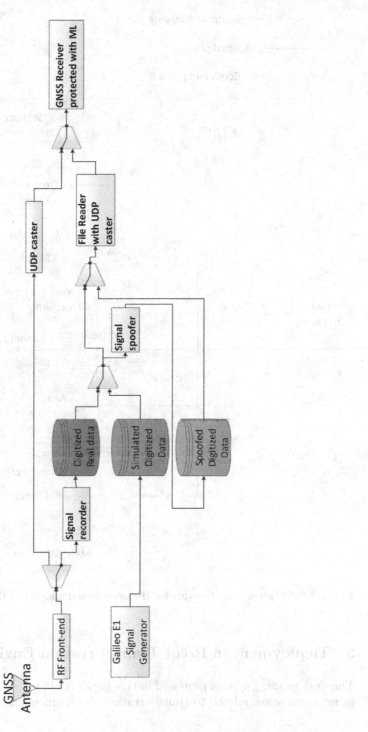

Fig. 1. GNSS spoofing workbench for operational deployment testing.

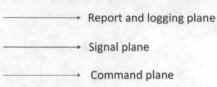

Report and logging plane

Signal plane

Command plane

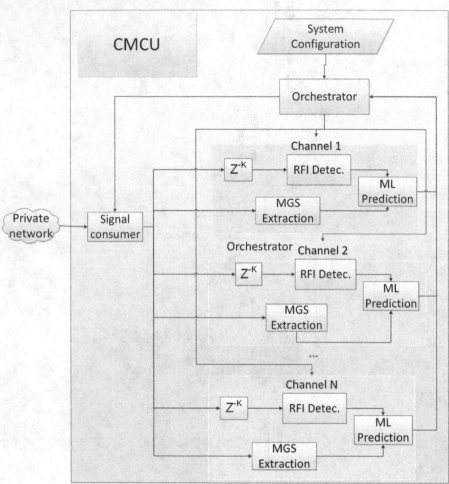

Fig. 2. CMCU algorithm structure for the operational instance of the protection system

3   Deployment in Road Transportation Environments

The anti-spoofing system proposed in this paper could be suitable to be deployed in next scenarios, related to transportation environments:

- **Areas of interest (Airports/Ports):** This application does not differ much with respect to the one originally conceived for the protection system, as long as the receiver antenna location is carefully picked to ensure open-sky conditions and low multipath. It has to be noted that the presence of frequent jammers in the ports/airports environment may increase the Probability of False Alarm (PFA), although it is not considered a risk, as the RFI presence is just one of the several inputs the protection system receives. The CMCU can be co-located in the ports/airports or centralized in a different location. The needed assumption of the antennas not being tampered with is easily met in this use case, as the airport/port authorities can ensure that the security means are provided for the antennas deployed in the port area. The value for an attacker of these two locations is clear, as the impact in the transportation means (either goods or people) may cause a considerable economical impact. Moreover, such attacks will be a critical point for autonomous operations of airplanes, vessels or cars operating in the area. Taking all into account, it could make sense that the authorities ensure the GNSS protection of such locations, where a convergence of large amount of road vehicles (e.g. cars, trucks, etc.) is expected. This includes the necessary alert means are provided in an autonomous manner, providing the surrounding users (or vehicles in a Machine to Machine communication, particularly for autonomous operations cases) with the assessment result from the CMCU operating in the port/airport. Cases of spoofing were reported in several ports already, like the one reported in [6], in the port of Vladivostok in 2017 and 2018, during the Eastern Economic Forum meeting in such city. The same document also informs about Spoofing cases in Gelendzhik Airport, the Sochi-Adler Airport, and the Vnukovo Airport in Moscow.
- **Roads with open-skies:** In the roads with an open-sky case, the deployment can be assimilated to the application case originally conceived for the protection system: An environment with open-sky and low multipath can be considered for this application. Clearly, an isolated instance of the protection system, with both the CMCU and the front end, is the proper configuration for such environment, as a dedicated high-bandwidth connection cannot be guaranteed. Note that a large truck is considered in this case, where enough computing capabilities can be installed and the antenna can be located in a location minimizing possible multipath. In this use case, the location of the antenna and its installation in the truck are also key to avoid self-spoofing attacks, as independent and auditable security means shall be put in place to protect the receiver and its antenna from being tampered (e.g. disconnecting the antenna to connect a signal generator). Examples of road spoofing events can be found in [6], like the event in Kerch in May, 2018. The very same application can be envisaged for large transportation vessels too, mainly for sea applications, as in-land waterways may be more challenging because of the expected GNSS outages and non-line-of-sight signals [5]. A large amount of examples of Spoofing attacks on vessels in the open sea justify the protection of maritime transportation means with the CMCU too. Examples can be found in [6], mainly discovered by analyzing the AIS data. Another

example of attacks to vessels in open sea can be found in [7], where the US Navy Arleigh Burke Class Guided Missile Destroyer was allegedly subject to a spoofing attack in June 2021 in the Crimea area.

– **Urban canyon areas:** This is the most challenging application, since multipath may degrade the expected results from the CMCU, as the solution was originally conceived to protect standoff receivers for critical applications. Therefore, in this case a two-fold solution is proposed: a CMCU would be located in the road vehicle, which would work only for overpowered signals (this is straightforward by training the ML algorithm with examples of SCER overpowered Spoofing attacks only) and, if clear sky locations are available in areas close to the urban canyon location, front ends shall be deployed around it, feeding a fixed CMCU trained with the full data set. The fixed CMCU may be operated by a local government or private organization, providing the assessment as a service. Similar automatic reporting systems, like the ones mentioned in the port/airport case, shall be put in place, providing the end users with the result of the fixed CMCU assessment, or, in case of autonomous operations, communicating the result to the autonomous road vehicles in a Machine to Machine communication. Thanks to the fixed CMCU, it is not only possible to protect the vehicles traveling along the road, but it is also possible to protect any system/application operating in the area (e.g. a mobile phone network, etc.). In the fixed CMCU, ensuring the tampering of the front end and the antenna is not taking place is more cumbersome, as there may be a large amount of front ends deployed in an area, feeding the fixed CMCU. This implies that security means (e.g. physical access control) shall be ensured in each one of the deployed antennas and front end, otherwise the security may be compromised (self-spoofed attack). On top of the physical access control, a proper monitor and control system, alerting of antenna disconnection events, shall be put in place. This would provide the needed means to ensure a proper security monitoring of the deployment.

4   Test Campaign with Real Signals

In order to test the operational setup with real signals but, at the same time, a controlled environment, signals in an open-sky environment were recorded.

The signals were later spoofed with a SCER MAP attack and recorded. Then, the spoofed and the original signals were pushed into the operational setup using the system outlined in Fig. 1, which allows the playback of a recorded signal and provides the operational setup with a signal via UDP network link. The samples are provided at the proper sample frequency, because the SW contains a throttle that pushes the samples at the proper rate to match a front end working at an specific sampling frequency.

The signals were recorded in the surroundings the Madrid area, on 08th of June, 2021 and 09th June, 2021 (exactly at Lat = 40.3560116, Lon = −4.3343342).

Two main test scenarios were provided to the platform: overpowered attack (i.e. the Spoofing attack is performed by providing a false signal that is received with more power than the real signal by the victim's receiver) and same-power attack (i.e. the false signal is received by the victim's receiver with a similar power with respect to the one received from the real satellite). The test scenarios are applicable for all the three identified road transportation use-cases.

The satellite used for testing was the Galileo satellite E33. It was received on ground during the tests with $C/N_0 \approx 40$ dBHz.

In order to make the tests more representative, the Machine Learning model loaded into the operational system was trained with data recorded on the same location on the 27th March at UTC 17:14 (approximately three months prior to the performed tests). A total of 134,474 data points were used to train the model. Out of the full of points, 40,343 were used to assess the expected theoretical performance, leaving to the Confusion Matrix in Table 1. The dataset was generated with E14 and spoofed overpowered signals and signals with similar power (with respect to the original signal) from the real records. The E14 had a $C/N_0 \approx 43$ dBHz.

As it can be seen in Fig. 3. The signals were recorded using a setup consisting of an USRP1 (Universal Software Radio Peripheral) and a computer running sending the samples via UDP connection to the CMCU. As it can be seen in Fig. 3.

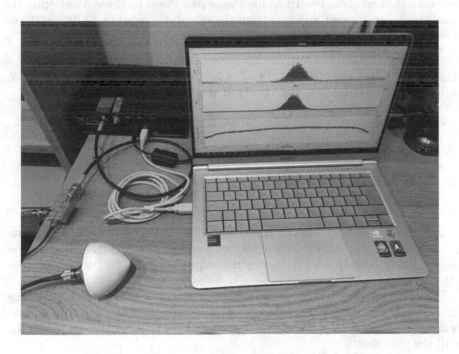

Fig. 3. USRP1 and computer used to record the data

In the case of the training dataset, for a subset of the overpowered spoofing cases, signals were placed on the exact same position in the victim's receiver search space. By doing that, a situation where an impossible signal, in terms of received power, was preventing the victim to identify two separate peaks was presented to the ML algorithm.

Table 1. Confusion Matrix for Decision Tree. 4 ms integration time with E1C PRN signal. No position fed to the algorithms. Expected performance of trained model with data from 27th March, 2021

Conf. matrix	True class	
	Spoofer present	*Spoofer not present*
Class. as Spoofer present	20,092	0
Class. as Spoofer not present	0	20,251

5   Results

For the testing of the operational system, no K-folds for training/testing was considered as necessary. The training part was performed with data recorded three months prior the operational test, as described in Sect. 4. Therefore, current tests with the prototype described here were performed by directly injecting the signals with and without Spoofers from the signals recorded on 08/06/2021 and 09/06/2021. The results can be found in Table 2.

Table 2. Confusion Matrix for Dec. Tree. 4 ms integration time with E1C PRN. No position fed to the algorithms. Results of test performed on June 2021

Conf. matrix	True class	
	Spoofer present	*Spoofer not present*
Class. as Spoofer present	430,000	0
Class. as Spoofer not present	0	430,000

The Spoofing dataset was composed of 215,000 data points with overpowered Spoofing signals and 215,000 data points with similar power to the original signal with E33. The Non-Spoofed dataset was composed of 430,000 data points from E33.

The results in other stages of the detection process inside of the CMCU (e.g. signal feature extraction) are nominal (i.e. performing according to the expected accuracy), as, unlike in the results in [1], the $C/N_0 \approx 40$ dBHz and was stable in all the recording.

Please note that, although the validation was performed offline, the signal was injected in the CMCU at the same pace that it would have been digested in a real time system.

The recording was also used to generate all the Spoofed cases.

This leads to a $PMD < 2.32 \times 10^{-6}$ and $PFA < 2.32 \times 10^{-6}$. Which is in line with the training dataset results, which pointed to $PMD < 10^{-4}$ and $PFA < 10^{-4}$.

Such results are of significant relevance as provide with a solid reliability baseline that enable the next steps in the process of generating a commercial product to protect road infrastructure that rely on GNSS.

Note that in a very dynamic situation, the expected results and performance will be negatively affected. This implies that special care should be taken with the signals used for training and the final setup, as per the remarks done in Sect. 3.

6   Conclusions

The work developed to implement the Operational protection system based on the theoretical system outlined in [1] was discussed. Its application in the road transportation market was reviewed. Performance results of the system with real Galileo signals were provided.

The results showed perfect detection for all tested cases, both for similar power spoofing attacks and overpowered spoofing attacks.

As described in Sect. 1.3 Neural Networks were discarded at an early stage in the analysis [1] because of its poor performance for the proposed cases, compared with the Decision Tree based algorithms. This is also substantiated by authors in [8,9] or [10] pointing to accuracy values around 1% of error.

Other proposed solutions, not based on ML algorithms, like [11], obtained important results ($PMD < 10^{-3}$ and $PFA < 10^{-3}$) with C/N_0 between 35 dBHz and 45 dBHz and a time to alarm of 1 s.

The proposed solution, based on the results obtained with the operational platform with real signals are $PMD < 2.32 \times 10^{-6}$ and $PFA < 2.32 \times 10^{-6}$ with $C/N_0 \approx 40$ dBHz and a time to alarm of 400 ms.

The time to alarm is expected to improve once the solution is deployed in a dedicated server, as the tests were performed with standard $\times 86$ machine with 8 vCPUs (Intel Core i7-10510U CPU@1.8 GHz) and 32 GB of RAM.

References

1. Gallardo, F., Pérez, A.: SCER spoofing attacks on the Galileo open service and machine learning techniques for end-user protection. IEEE Access 8, 85515–85532 (2020). https://doi.org/10.1109/ACCESS.2020.2992119
2. Humphreys, E.: Assessing the spoofing threat: Development of a portable GPS civilian spoofer. In: Proceedings 21th International Technical Meeting Satellite Division Institute Navigation (ION), Savannah, GA, USA (2008)

3. Caparra, G.: On the achievable equivalent security of GNSS ranging code encryption. In: Proceedings IEEE/ION Position Location Navigation Symposium (PLANS), Monterey, CA, USA, pp. 956–966 (2018)
4. Ivezic, Z., Connolly, A.J., VanderPlas, J.T., Gray, A.: Statistics, Data Mining, and Machine Learning in Astronomy: A Practical Python Guide for the Analysis of Survey Data. Princeton University Press, Princeton (2014)
5. Medina, D.A., Romanovas, M., Herrera-Pinzón, I., Ziebold, R.: Robust position and velocity estimation methods in integrated navigation systems for inland water applications. In: IEEE/ION Position, Location and Navigation Symposium (PLANS), pp. 491–501 (2016). https://doi.org/10.1109/PLANS.2016.7479737
6. C4ADS: Above Us Only Stars. 1st edn. Publisher, Washington, USA (2019)
7. Resilient Navigation and Timing Foundation. https://rntfnd.org/2021/06/30/u-s-navy-ship-spoofed-to-crimea/. Accessed 6 July 2021
8. Shafiee, E., Mosavi, M., Moazedi, M.: Detection of spoofing attack using machine learning based on multi-layer neural network in single-frequency GPS receivers. J. Navig. **71**(1), 169–188 (2017). https://doi.org/10.1017/S0373463317000558
9. Manesh, M.R., Kenney, J., Hu, W.C., Devabhaktuni, V.K., Kaabouch N.: Detection of GPS spoofing attacks on unmanned aerial systems. In: 16th IEEE Annual Consumer Communications and Networking Conference (CCNC), Las Vegas, NV, USA, pp. 1–6 (2019). https://doi.org/10.1109/CCNC.2019.8651804
10. Shafique A., Mehmood A and Elhadef M.: Detecting Signal Spoofing Attack in UAVs Using Machine Learning Models. In: IEEE Access, https://doi.org/10.1109/ACCESS.2021.3089847
11. Turner M., Wimbush S., Enneking C., Konovaltsev A.: Spoofing detection by distortion of the correlation function. In: IEEE/ION Position, Location and Navigation Symposium (PLANS), Portland, OR, USA, pp. 566–574 (2020). https://doi.org/10.1109/PLANS46316.2020.9110173

Deployment and Simulation of a Real ITS-G5 Implementation

Nagore Iturbe-Olleta[1,2(✉)], Jon Bilbao[1,2], Jon Amengual[1,2], Alfonso Brazalez[1,2], and Jaizki Mendizabal[1,2]

[1] Ceit Basque Research and Technology Alliance (BRTA), Manuel Lardizabal 15, 20018 Donostia/San Sebastián, Spain
niturbe@ceit.es
[2] Universidad de Navarra, Tecnun, Manuel Lardizabal 13, 20018 Donostia/San Sebastián, Spain

Abstract. Due to the fact of the increasing necessity and demands of the vehicle to everything communications (V2X), which includes vehicle to vehicle (V2V) and vehicle to infrastructure (V2I) communications, new communication technologies need to be deployed and tested in real environments. Moreover, Cooperative Awareness Messages (CAM) and Decentralised Environmental Notification Messages (DENM) should be analysed and understood so as to determine which type of message should be sent when a specific alert has to be transmitted. In this paper, a communication schema with the ability to manage alerts generated in a Traffic Control Center, transforming them to the corresponding DENM messages and sending them to the required roadside unit (RSU) will be explained and tested in a real deployment scenario. In addition to this, to be able to easily test different scenarios of future real deployments a simulation of it will be explained that will help to create more specific scenarios and implement improvements without further cost or delay with the conclusion that the simulation tool needs more development to appropiately test V2X communications in real environments.

Keywords: ITS-G5 · Deployment · Simulation · V2V · V2I · V2X

1 Introduction

In the last years, road safety improvement and efficient road traffic management have been some of the main objectives of the automotive industry and the governments. One of the enablers to achieve these objectives will be the wireless communication systems, that have been developing over the years. The idea of making the vehicles communicate with each other, Vehicle to Vehicle communication (V2V), or with a nearby infrastructure, Vehicle to Infrastructure communication (V2I), is becoming a reality. The method by which the vehicles can communicate with everything (V2X) is part of the Intelligent Transport Systems (ITS).

J. Moreno García-Loygorri et al. (Eds.): Nets4Cars/Nets4Trains/Nets4Aircraft 2021, LNCS 13120, pp. 27–36, 2021.
https://doi.org/10.1007/978-3-030-92684-7_3

One of the communication standards for V2I and V2X is the IEEE 802.11p [1]. To implement this type of communication two devices are particularly used, RoadSide Units (RSU) that are deployed in infrastructures and Onboard Units (OBU) located in vehicles. The RSUs installed on the infrastructures communicate with OBUs that are located in vehicles that circulate near the RSUs, this way a vehicle is capable of communicating with a RSU (V2I). Moreover, vehicles can communicate with other OBUs (V2V) through the RSU or directly without the need of it.

Nowadays, there are some V2X simulators to help develop real V2X communication scenarios Veins being the most famous one. But most of the simulators only simulate small areas like cities as can be seen in [2], however, VANET (Vehicular Ad hoc NETwork) networks need to be deployed in larger areas like provinces in Spain and the simulation tools need to offer more capabilities to simulate those behaviours, not only in terms of scalability but also in terms of the OSI (Open Systems Interconnection) levels as Veins does not reach the application level. A new simulator has now emerged called Artery which started as an extension of Veins [3] but can now be used independently [4], Artery reaches the facility layer and enables the inclusion of new message types if needed.

This paper is structured as follows:

- Section 2 explains the deployment of a real ITS-G5 infrastructure
- Secion 3 explains the simulation of the communication infrastructure
- Secion 4 presents the simulation of the physical environment
- Secion 5 shows the results
- Secion 6 shows the conclusions.

2   Deployment of a Real ITS-G5 Infrastructure in A8-E15

A real ITS-G5 deployment consists on the installation, in a real road environment, of RSUs that are capable of receiving traffic alerts and sending them through the ITS-G5 standard to nearby OBUs. For that purpose, a real implementation of the V2X communications has been made in the province of Bizkaia in Spain, 6 RSUs have been placed over the A-8 highway so that most of that highway is covered. But before the deployment takes place some key points need to be addressed.

One of the key aspects is the location of the RSUs. Usually, their location is not "freely" decided as some factors can clearly alter that decision. To install a RSU, there is a need for an infrastructure with electricity where they can be placed and the corresponding permission of the owner of the infrastructure is also required.

The connectivity with five of the RSUs is made by a router, which would be later explained, and another RSU is communicated by fibre optics. Moreover, one RSU is placed near a toll so that the interference is tracked. Taking into consideration all the aforementioned aspects, the following locations were chosen:

- El Haya (43°20′29.72″ N 3°09′00.86″ O)
- Max Center (43°17′19.10″ N 3°00′18.27″ O)
- Peñaskal (43°14′17.65″ N 2°56′49.39″ O)

- Erletxes (43°13'54.08" N 2°47'00.57" O)
- Gerediaga (43°10'23.86" N 2°36'50.48" O)
- Zaldibar (43°10'03.51" N 2°32'47.22" O).

The following image shows the ubications in a real map, 6 RSUs were installed over 50 km (Fig. 1):

Fig. 1. ITS-G5 deployment ubication

Another key aspect is the communication to the field RSUs as the RSUs could need some fix, the code could need to be updated... For that, the solution in our case has been to install a Cohda MK5 RSU with a Teltonika RUT240 router. With the router, remote access to the RSU is guaranteed not only for monitoring the RSU but also to be able to make the RSU send the required messages.

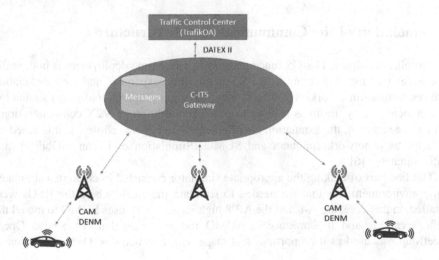

Fig. 2. ITS-G5 deployment architecture

The architecture of the system is as follows (Fig. 2):

The central part of the communication system is the Gateway which works the following way. The Gateway implements an OPC-UA (Object linking and embedding for Process Control Unified Architecture) server that receives the alerts coming from the Traffic Control Center, those alerts are in DATEX II format that is the language used in Europe for the exchange of traffic information and traffic data [5]. The Gateway processes the DATEX II alerts and transforms them into C-ITS (Cooperative-ITS) messages, more precisely in DENM messages depending on the alert type. Currently, the Gateway can process the following alerts (Table 1):

Table 1. DATEX II to DENM

DATEX II		DENM (ETSI EN 302 637-3)	
Class	Type	Cause code	Subcause code
PoorEnvironmentConditions	Fog	18	1
PoorEnvironmentConditions	Rain	19	1
WeatherRelatedRoadConditions	Black ice	6	6
Congested road	Traffic condition	1	3
MaintenanceWorks	Maintenance work	3	0
Road operator service disruption	Incidents	14	1
Accident	Stationary vehicle	2	0

Once the alert is transformed into the corresponding DENM message, the latitude and the longitude of the alert is obtained and the DENM message is sent to the RSU that is closest to where the alert is occurring. The Gateway is also capable of cancelling DENMs so when a cancellation alert is received from the Traffic Control Center with the id of the message, the Gateway searches in the database which RSU is sending the alert with the corresponding id and proceeds to its cancellation.

3   Simulation of the Communication Infrastructure

The installation of new ITS-G5 functionalities in a real time deployment is both really expensive and time consuming as the RSUs are quite expensive and their installation requires permissions, workers... That is why, having a properly configured simulation environment is very useful as it helps to develop and improve V2X communications. After some research, the simulation environment "Artery" was chosen as it is based on Omnetpp as a network simulator and SUMO (Simulation of Urban MObility) as a traffic simulator [6].

The first part of making the appropriate simulator consisted in creating a simulated traffic environment, for that we needed to simulate the roads where the RSUs were installed, in this case, the A-8 and the AP-8 highways. Artery uses SUMO to model the traffic scenarios and to introduce in SUMO the real map that we needed OpenStreetMap was used as it proportions real maps with free licenses. Once the region of interest of our map was selected and downloaded a problem occurred, SUMO is only capable of handling sizes of that of a city but in our case, our region included an entire county so the quantity of data had to be reduced. For that, information on the map that was not necessary was deleted like secondary roads, cities, mountains... On the following images, a map of the roads and the simulated road is presented and as it can be seen they are identical (Figs. 3 and 4).

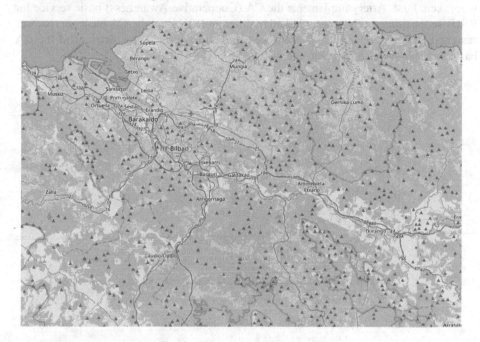

Fig. 3. Real A-8 and AP-8 roads

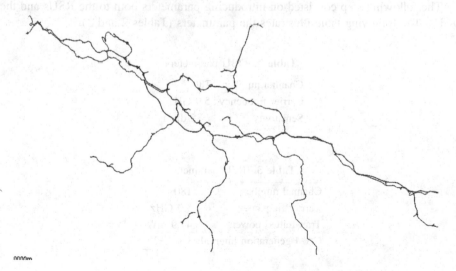

Fig. 4. Simulation of A-8 and AP-8 roads in SUMO

Then, the RSUs were located in the map, unfortunately, SUMO does not have an "RSU" object type so instead POI (Point of Interest) object type was used. The map maintains the real latitude and longitude of the RSUs so the location of the RSUs was relatively straightforward. For the OBU, cars were introduced in the simulation, each with a specific route that involves one or more RSUs in the way.

To be able to simulate the real time scenario's network side the following approach was taken. First, Artery implements the CA (Cooperative Awareness) basic service for RSUs so the different POIs were linked to different RSUs and the CA basic service was assigned to them, vehicles in SUMO were linked to vehicles on Artery and the CA basic service was also added to them (Fig. 5).

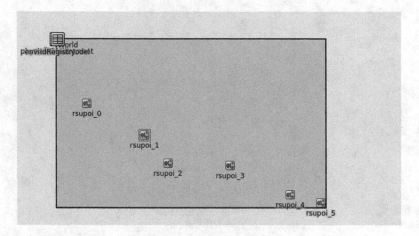

Fig. 5. Network simulation

The following step consisted on introducing parameters both to the RSUs and the OBUs. The following table illustrates the parameters (Tables 2 and 3):

Table 2. OBU parameters

Channel number	180
Carrier frequency	5.9 GHz
Sensitivity	−85 dBm

Table 3. RSU parameters

Channel number	180
Carrier frequency	5.9 GHz
Transmitted power	47.9 mW
CAM generation interval	1 s

4 Simulation of the Physical Environment

Artery gives the ability to improve the simulations as it is based on Omnetpp. The main characteristic is the ability to simulate a real physical environment as it uses the INET library, for the physical environment characteristics data obtained from the real deployment were used. From the tests obtained of the real deployment our RSUs started and stopped receiving C-ITS messages at the following points, the green points are where the signal is received (both ways are shown), the yellow points are where the signal stopped being received and the red circle has a radius of 500 m (Figs. 6 and 7).

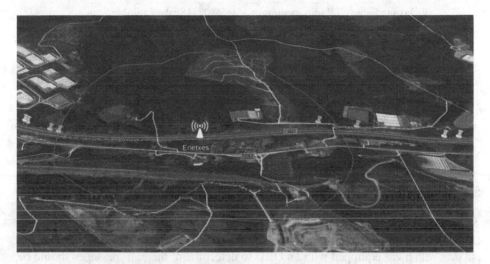

Fig. 6. Communication range of the RSU of Erletxes (Color figure online)

Fig. 7. Communication range of the RSU of Gerediaga (Color figure online)

As it is shown in the images due to the complex orography that exists in the area of the deployment, the messages sent by the RSUs were only received by the OBU in an area of more or less 500 m. That is why, that was the value set as the maximum communication range of the radio medium, there is a small GPS error but, overall, the RSUs give a good coverage area.

The following values were also introduced considering the physical characteristics of the real deployment scenario (Table 4):

Table 4. Physical characteristics

Radio medium	Radio medium	ieee80211ScalarRadioMedium
	Propagation type	ConstantSpeedPropagation
	Path loss type	Gemv2
	Obstacle loss	–
	AnalogModelType	IsotropicScalarBackgroundNoise
Propagation	Propagation speed	2.99792e+08 mps
Analog model	AnalogModel	ScalarAnalogModel
BackgroundNoise	Background noise	IsotropicScalarBackgroundNoise

5   Results

A Demo test was carried out in the real deployment with the RSUs of Erletxes and Gerediaga, this Demo consisted in activating specific messages on both RSUs and passing with a car equipped with an OBU to detect them; then all messages should be cancelled and on the way back other messages should be activated and the vehicle with the OBU should detect them again.

On the first way, two DENM messages were activated in the RSU of Erletxes, specifically fog and stationary vehicle alerts, and an alert of rain was activated in the RSU of Gerediaga. Later both alerts were cancelled, and a message of rain was activated in Gerediaga and a message of a traffic jam ahead in Erletxes.

The results were the following: The RSUs by the specification of the manufacturer have a propagation range of various kilometers but as the orography of the Basque Country is very mountainous the real propagation range was of 500 m approximately in every direction. Moreover, the packets that were received by the OBU had a propagation delay of 2 ms, which is expected in vehicular communications but there existed a significant amount of packet loss on either RSUs on both ways.

In Erletxes with the first two messages, there was a packet loss of 80.01% and on the other way of 14,29%, in Gerediaga on the first way, the packet loss was 15,79% and on the other way of 94,67%. This packet loss should be further analyzed with the help of the simulation tool to improve the overall performance of the real ITS-G5 deployment. Regarding CAM messages, which are always sent, firstly in Erletxes, the packet loss was 80.05% and on the other way of 20%; in Gerediaga on the first way the packet loss was 2.13% and on the other way of 20%.

A simulation of the Demo was carried out to compare the results, our simulation consisted on two vehicles each one equipped with an OBU, the first vehicle did the route from Erletxes to Gerediaga and the second vehicle did the route from Gerediaga to Erletxes. The messages sent were generic CAM messages, but the results differ from the ones of the real Demo (Figs. 8 and 9):

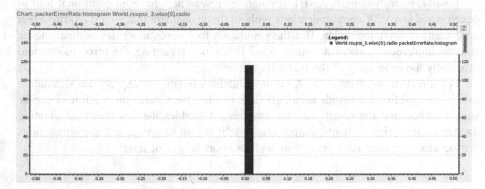

Fig. 8. RSU Erletxes packet error rate histogram

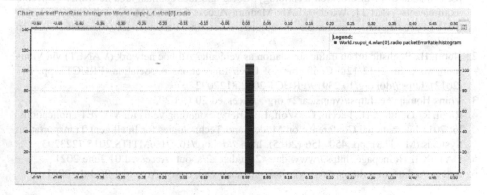

Fig. 9. RSU Gerediaga packet error rate histogram

As the graphics show the error rate on both RSUs is 0, this is because the error model of the simulation needs to be improved as well as the orography of the real environment implemented.

As for the messages, the RSU of Erletxes sent on the first way 319 messages and all of them were received by the OBU, and the second time of the 259 messages sent the 259 messages were received. In Gerediaga, the first time the vehicle approached the RSU of the 289 messages sent, 289 were received and the second time from the 329 messages sent 329 were received. This 100% of message reception is also explained due to a lack of a proper error model.

6 Conclusions

With the presented approach for carrying a real ITS-G5 deployment, a communication schema was developed so that the alerts generated in a Traffic Control Center reach the required RSU with the specified DENM message. Moreover, the results of a Demo of the deployment were presented with an explanation of the improvements needed.

Finally, with dynamic VANET simulations researchers have an additional tool to develop and test V2X communications without the investment that would require a real time scenario implementation. But the simulation tool needs more development to be able to implement a more adequate RSU behaviour regarding the error model and especially the orography of the real environment.

For a real deployment of V2X communications having an appropriate simulation tool is very useful as it avoids accidents (loss of life), the simulation conditions can be varied ad-hoc and the results can be analyzed, it enables the possibility of creating dangerous scenarios without creating real risk, it is cost-effective, and the simulations can be analyzed over long periods as well as short ranges of time.

1. References

1. IEEE Standard for Information technology: Local and metropolitan area networks—Specific requirements—Part 11: Wireless LAN Medium Access Control (MAC) and Physical Layer (PHY) Specifications Amendment 6: Wireless Access in Vehicular Environments, 802.11p (2010)
2. Noori, H.: Realistic urban traffic simulation as vehicular Ad-hoc network (VANET) via Veins framework. In: 2012 12th Conference of Open Innovations Association (FRUCT), pp. 1–7 (2012). https://doi.org/10.23919/FRUCT.2012.8122092
3. Veins Homepage. https://veins.car2x.org/. Accessed 20 Oct 2021
4. Riebl, R., Günther, H., Facchi, C., Wolf, L.: Artery: extending veins for VANET applications. In: 2015 International Conference on Models and Technologies for Intelligent Transportation Systems (MT-ITS), pp. 450–456 (2015). https://doi.org/10.1109/MTITS.2015.7223293
5. DATEX II Homepage. https://www.datex2.eu/datex2/about. Accessed 01 June 2021
6. Artery Architecture. http://artery.v2x-research.eu/architecture/. Accessed 06 July 2021

Towards an Adaptive Blockchain
for Internet of Vehicles

Leo Mendiboure$^{(\boxtimes)}$, Sassi Maaloul, and Hasnaa Aniss

COSYS/ERENA Lab, University Gustave Eiffel, Bordeaux, France
{leo.mendiboure,sassi.maaloul2,hasnaa.aniss}@univ-eiffel.fr

Abstract. Cybersecurity is an essential requirement to enable the deployment of Cooperative-Intelligent Transportation Systems (C-ITS). In vehicular networks, Blockchain is a solution often considered to secure exchanges between nodes. In fact, this technology could enable each vehicle to check by itself the content of each message it receives, without the need to trust its neighbors. Nevertheless, Blockchain was initially designed for wired networks. Therefore, its deployment in vehicular networks would imply considering the features of this environment: high mobility, variable C-ITS applications' requirements, limited vehicles capabilities, etc. That is why, in this paper, after comparing existing solutions, we introduce a new adaptive Blockchain framework, designed to address the vehicular environment challenges. We also describe a Blockchain architecture that could support this framework and present future directions that will contribute to its implementation and evaluation.

Keywords: Internet of Vehicles (IoV) · C-ITS · Cybersecurity · Blockchain · Adaptive · Consensus · Quality of service · AI · Energy efficiency

1 Introduction

The Internet of Vehicles (IoV) paradigm, in vehicular networks, is becoming more and more important today [26]. In fact, the IoV architecture could enable vehicles to communicate with each other efficiently and with their environment thanks to the integration of different technologies, including Software Defined Networking and 5G cellular networks [28].

In particular, IoV could support essential services for connected and automated vehicles: Cooperative Intelligent Transport Systems (C-ITS) [6]. C-ITS, by enabling the exchange of information related to vehicles' behavior (hard breaking, lane changing, etc.) and environment (obstacle detection, pedestrian detection, etc.) aim to improve both road safety and traffic efficiency. However, C-ITS will only enhance road safety if the communications between vehicles are secure. Indeed, if a malicious entity (vehicle, roadside equipment, etc.) was able to transmit erroneous information, C-ITS could actually increase the level of insecurity.

© Springer Nature Switzerland AG 2021
J. Moreno García-Loygorri et al. (Eds.): Nets4Cars/Nets4Trains/Nets4Aircraft 2021, LNCS 13120, pp. 37–48, 2021.
https://doi.org/10.1007/978-3-030-92684-7_4

That is why, many researchers are currently trying to define solutions to secure vehicular networks. To authenticate and control the access of vehicles, and thus to check their identity, different standardized architectures, based on a Public Key Infrastructure (PKI), have already been proposed [16]. Nevertheless, even an authenticated entity could be malicious and spread misinformation. That is why, checking the reliability of the messages, to reinforce the trust between vehicles, is another crucial issue [10].

Blockchain technology [21], a popular distributed ledger technology, based on a Peer-to-Peer (P2P) network and a consensus algorithm, could be a way to achieve that [17]. Indeed, this technology is designed to enable the secure exchange of information between nodes. It could allow each vehicle to check by itself the content of each message it receives, without the need to trust its neighbors (distributed ledger). This corresponds perfectly to a situation where it is impossible to know if and which vehicles are malicious. Consequently, the Blockchain approach appears to be an interesting way to improve security in vehicular networks.

However, this technology was initially designed for wired networks. Therefore, its deployment in vehicular network would require taking into account high level of mobility of vehicles and limited lifetime of communication links. Beyond that, it might also be necessary to take into account the diverse requirements of C-ITS applications (Quality of Service, security, etc.), user preferences (privacy) as well as the fluctuating capabilities of vehicles (energy, storage, communication, etc.). Thus, to be applied in IoV and C-ITS, the Blockchain will have to be adaptive [13].

To date, the issues related to the adaptation of the Blockchain technology to the vehicular context have not been sufficiently addressed in the literature [19]. Indeed, many papers directly apply this technology without discussing its limitations. Therefore, in this paper, we introduce a new Blockchain framework, adapted both to the vehicular context (mobility, link lifetime), and to the C-ITS application requirements, user preferences and vehicle capabilities. The main contributions of this paper are:

- A comparison of the state-of-the-art solutions aiming to integrate the Blockchain technology into the IoV environment;
- The identification of design requirements as well as an architecture and technological tools that could contribute to the definition of an optimal Blockchain framework for IoV;
- A presentation of future directions that will allow the implementation of this adaptive Blockchain framework.

The rest of this paper is organized as follows: Sect. 2 compares the state-of-the-art solutions aiming to enable the deployment of the Blockchain technology in IoV and C-ITS. Then, Sect. 3 introduces the proposed adaptive Blockchain framework. Finally, the main challenges related to the deployment of this framework are tackled in Sect. 4.

2   Related Work

In this section, we present the main research papers that focused on the definition of an adaptive Blockchain for vehicular networks (cf. Sect. 2.1). We also argue for the definition of a new, adaptable and global Blockchain framework for IoV and C-ITS (cf. Sect. 2.2).

2.1   State-of-the-Art Solutions

As stated in the introduction, a Blockchain framework designed for vehicular networks should take into account the vehicular context (mobility, links lifetime, etc.), the diverse requirements of C-ITS applications (Quality of Service, security, etc.), the user preferences (privacy) and the fluctuating capabilities of vehicles (energy, storage, communication, etc.).

- Vehicular Context: Regarding the adaptation of the Blockchain technology to the vehicular networks' characteristics (link lifetime, high mobility), an idea that is being highly studied today is to consider local Blockchain networks. These local ledgers (micro-Blockchain) could be used to enable vehicles located within the same area to exchange information while abstracting their mobility. However, this solution, first introduced in [4], was defined without considering vehicular applications' requirements: Quality of Service, information distribution area, etc. Therefore, this idea cannot be applied to C-ITS services;
- Application Requirements: Regarding applications, existing works can be divided into two categories, security-related papers such as [11, 27] and Quality of service-related papers such as [12,14,24]. These works are relevant in their field, as they attempt to improve both the security and the Quality of Service of a Blockchain framework in vehicular networks. However, they have the same limitation: they do not aim to adapt the performance level (security, Quality of Service) to the application requirements but to maximize them. A maximum level of security and a maximum level of Quality of Service are not required for all applications and could lead to significant additional costs: energy, computing, communication, etc. Therefore, these works propose only a partial and non-optimal solution;
- User Preferences: Blockchain frameworks, designed for vehicular networks, have not addressed this user preference awareness so far. Indeed, privacy-preserving trust models, such as [15], do not take into account user preferences as they only aim to enhance privacy. Therefore, this idea still needs to be explored;
- Vehicle Capabilities: The main goal of the studies focusing on this point is to improve the performance of the Blockchain network by selecting only Blockchain nodes that can guarantee a high processing and communication capacity [14,24]. Indeed, this could reduce latency and improve throughput. However, such a selection process could lead to an overload of these nodes in some situations (important quantity of information exchanged). Therefore, it

would be important to propose other mechanisms to use a more significant number of nodes and balance energy consumption and computation load.

2.2 Positioning

Table 1. Comparison of the different vehicular architectures

Params. Prop.	Vehicular context	Applications requirements	User preferences	Vehicle capabilities
[4]	Partial	No	No	No
[11]	No	Partial	No	No
[27]	No	Partial	No	No
[12]	No	Partial	No	No
[14]	No	Partial	No	Partial
[24]	No	Partial	No	Partial
Proposition	Yes	Yes	Yes	Yes

Various papers have already been proposed in the literature to improve vehicular networks security thanks to the Blockchain technology (see Sect. 2.1). As can be seen in Table 1, these papers aimed to adapt the Blockchain technology to the vehicular context [4], to the C-ITS applications requirements [11,12,14,24,27] and to the vehicles capabilities [14,24].

However, these issues (applications requirements, vehicle capabilities, vehicular context) have only been partially addressed. Indeed, state-of-the-art papers have tried to maximize Blockchain performance rather than to adapt Blockchain to the actual requirements of Blockchain applications. Therefore, the proposed solutions could result in significant overheads. Moreover, none of the solutions proposed so far simultaneously meets these three objectives (vehicular context, applications requirements, vehicles capabilities). Finally, user preferences have not been considered so far in these different Blockchain frameworks.

That's why, in this paper, we introduce a new Blockchain framework for IoV and C-ITS. This framework aims to take into account both vehicular context, C-ITS application requirements, user preferences and vehicle capabilities.

3   An Adaptive Blockchain Framework for Vehicular Network

In this section, we introduce a Blockchain framework designed to secure vehicular networks. It aims to address the discussed limitations (see Sect. 2) and to offer a forward-looking solution for Blockchain-based vehicular systems.

3.1 Design Requirements

As indicated in the introduction of this paper, we have identified four key points characterizing the IoV and C-ITS basic requirements. To be efficiently applied in vehicular networks, the proposed Blockchain framework, will have to address:

- **Vehicular Context:** The vehicular environment is characterized by a high level of mobility of the nodes and a short lifetime of the communication links. The proposed Blockchain framework will have to take into account these characteristics. It will have to guarantee an efficient distribution of information despite this mobility. In particular, it will be necessary to guarantee the real-time distribution of critical information related to road safety, and consequently, to enable an efficient information prioritization;
- **Applications Requirements:** C-ITS applications have a large range of Quality of Service and security requirements. Therefore, the proposed framework must adapt data distribution to applications' requirements (different Quality of Service and security levels). To enable that, this framework will require information related to C-ITS applications (expected performance), real-time network state (real-time performance) and real-time Blockchain nodes' state;
- **User Preferences:** The proposed Blockchain framework will have to take into account the users' preferences. This could correspond to the level of privacy protection expected by this user or to his involvement in the verification and validation process of the information stored in the Blockchain ledger. Other points can also be defined. These users preferences will have to be stored in a Blockchain ledger;
- **Vehicle Capabilities:** Vehicles are mobile nodes and they necessarily have a limited capacity (storage, calculation, communication, energy). The proposed Blockchain framework must consider this factor and the load associated with data validation and storage must be efficiently distributed among the different Blockchain nodes. Mechanisms will have to be implemented to guarantee the framework's operation even if a Blockchain node is overloaded or crashes. In addition, the consensus algorithm used by the Blockchain framework will have to guarantee a high level of energy efficiency.

3.2 Proposed Blockchain Architecture

The architecture proposed to implement this framework extends the one we introduced in [18] and aims to provide a higher level of adaptation. This architecture, shown in Fig. 1, has three main characteristics:

- **Different Types of Blockchain Nodes are Considered:** Unlike what we proposed in [18], here, we consider both full and light Blockchain nodes to improve Blockchain network's performance. Full nodes are Blockchain nodes that participate in both data validation and data storage. Light nodes only have data access (they have a copy of the Blockchain ledger) and do not

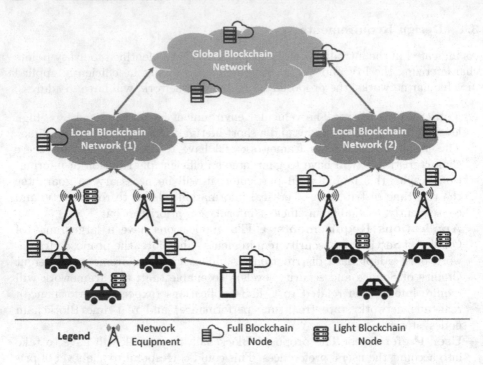

Fig. 1. Proposed blockchain architecture for IoV

participate in the data validation process. These lightweight nodes could be used to take into account the capacity of different Blockchain nodes. Indeed, some vehicles could have enough storage capacity to store the Blockchain ledger but insufficient computing capacity to verify its reliability. Thus, by using these vehicles as light Blockchain nodes, it might be possible to enhance the data availability level without overloading them;

- **Different Equipments are Considered to Host these Blockchain Nodes:** This is also a significant improvement compared to what we proposed in [18], that could enable a higher level of scalability. We consider that Blockchain nodes could be hosted by vehicles, but also by other User Equipments (UE) that could be integrated in the Internet of Vehicles (smartphones, surveillance cameras, etc.), by network equipments (Base Stations, Road Side Units) and also by remote servers (cloud servers). Such an architecture could be a way to take advantage of all available nodes' capabilities (computation, storage, communication, energy). We could therefore imagine positioning the verification and data storage functionalities at optimal locations according to the specific requirements of each C-ITS application. We could also consider using different types of nodes depending on the expected level of security;
- **A Multi-level Blockchain Structure is Considered:** We consider a sub-network decomposition of the Blockchain architecture. Depending on the requirements of each C-ITS application and the vehicular density, a street,

a city or a region could be considered as a sub-network (see Fig. 1: Local Blockchain Network). As we demonstrated in [18], such an architecture could significantly improve the level of scalability of the Blockchain architecture: maximum throughput, reduced latency, etc. Moreover, this architecture could be used to optimize the data storage/verification process and to transmit a given information only to relevant Blockchain nodes (located within a same geographical area).

It can be noted that this architecture also has common features with the architecture we proposed in [18]:

- First, the Blockchain network is considered as a public network and all IoV nodes can be involved in this network (both for reading and validating data). The Blockchain is primarily seen as an alternative way of securing exchanges between vehicles (and other IoV nodes);
- Then, the authentication of Blockchain nodes is based on a traditional Public Key Infrastructure (PKI). The architecture usually used for certificate generation in C-ITS could be used to generate certificates for Blockchain nodes. This solution could also enable pseudonyms generation for these nodes and thus enhance user privacy;
- Thereafter, for inter-Blockchain networks' communications (locals and global Blockchain), solutions such as *channels* [2] used by Hyperledger Fabric, a popular Blockchain implementation [1], could be considered (cf our implementation in [18]). This could allow a simplified exchange of information between these sub-networks;
- Finally, regarding evaluation, tools such as Mininet-WiFi could be considered [7]. Indeed, it could be used to emulate Blockchain nodes while taking into account the mobility of the vehicular environment thanks to Simulation of Urban MObility (SUMO) [3]. Regarding the Blockchain itself, for simple improvements of existing systems, as we have already done in [18], Hyperledger Fabric or Hyperledger Iroha could be considered. Different types of evaluations could be carried out, in particular, the performance gain of the proposed solution compared to state-of-the-art approaches in terms of communication overhead, latency or Blockchain nodes' CPU usage. It could also be interesting to evaluate the system's ability to deal with cyber-attacks (percentage of malicious nodes supported).

3.3   Considered Solutions to Meet Design Requirements

To meet the design requirements identified in Sect. 3.1, different solutions could be considered. Some of these mechanisms are presented in this section.

Vehicular Context. To enable the Blockchain framework to operate in a highly mobile environment, the use of finite-time and fixed-time consensus algorithms would be an interesting approach [9]. Indeed, this could be used to calculate the time required to validate and disseminate a given piece of information. Therefore, combining this information with vehicles data (speed, position, direction, etc.), it would be possible to determine in real time to which vehicles a given information could be transmitted. It could also be interesting to determine an optimal value for the consensus duration depending on the network topology and the requirements of the concerned C-ITS application. Another important element in mobility management is the use of network equipments as Blockchain nodes (cf. Fig. 1). Indeed, as they are fixed nodes, they could be used to transmit information to a larger number of vehicles or to nearby roadside equipments. Adaptive consensus and optimal use of available Blockchain nodes therefore seem to be two critical factors for the deployment of a Blockchain framework in vehicular networks.

Applications Requirements. To meet the requirements of a wide range of applications, a first important parameter seems to be to be able to adapt the structure of the chain of blocks to each application [25]. Indeed, different applications may require a different structure of data as well as a variable access to these data. Similarly, different applications may require separate consensus. Indeed, depending on the type of data, different steps may be necessary: simple verification in the Blockchain ledger, matching of data from different vehicles, etc. Then, depending on the Quality of Service requirements of the applications, it may be necessary to adapt the duration of the consensus [8,9]. Indeed, reducing this duration could improve throughput and reduce latency. However, increasing this performance level might result in a lower level of security. When the consensus duration is reduced, the number of nodes participating in the consensus is also reduced. This could facilitate malicious behavior. Therefore, it will be essential to find a trade-off between performance and security to ensure the proper functioning of C-ITS applications. To achieve this, it would be possible to determine, in each situation, an optimal number of nodes participating in the verification process. Based on that, it would be possible to calculate a realistic consensus duration. Another way to increase security could be to define for each Blockchain node a trust index (based on its past behavior) [22]. Then, this index could be used to select only reliable nodes for the Blockchain verification process. Therefore, to meet applications requirements, an adaptive consensus, a dynamic data structure and a trade-off between security and performance seem to be three important factors.

User Preferences. Taking into account user preferences is perhaps the simplest issue to address. Indeed, to enable that, the Blockchain framework should integrate an interface allowing each user to interact with the Blockchain ledger. This interface should, in particular, offer this user the possibility to modify various parameters such as the expected level of privacy. The only critical point for this user preference management would be to store securely, and anonymously, the data related to each user. It would also be important to determine the different parameters that each user could modify.

Vehicle Capabilities. To take into account the variable and limited capacity of each vehicle, a first obvious solution would be to distribute the workload fairly among the different Blockchain nodes. This will necessarily reduce the probability of overloading each node. To go further, a complementary solution would be to adapt the behavior of the Blockchain to the requirements of each C-ITS application and to the real-time capabilities of the Blockchain nodes. Some consensus algorithms can significantly reduce the amount of energy required to verify data [23]. Therefore, a "minimal" consensus should be selected for each application to ensure the proper functioning of this application while reducing the energy footprint. It could also be interesting to optimally use the available Blockchain nodes' capabilities. Indeed, fixed nodes (cloud, network equipment) have higher capacities: storage, calculation, energy, etc. Therefore, these nodes could be used for longer-term storage of larger amounts of information, while vehicles could be used for instant verification of information and for short-term storage of this information. Thus, fair load balancing, consensus adaptability and data storage adaptability are three key factors to deal with vehicle capabilities.

4   Future Directions

The ideas introduced in this paper should enable the implementation of an adaptive Blockchain framework designed for vehicular networks. However, to deploy this framework, various challenges still need to be addressed.

4.1   An Efficient Decision Making Process

To ensure the adaptability of the Blockchain framework to the vehicular context, to the C-ITS applications' requirements and to the vehicles' varying capabilities, the use of decision making support tools seems to be essential (cf. Sect. 3.3). Artificial Intelligence (AI) techniques (machine learning, deep learning, etc.) are now widely studied in vehicular networks [20]. Indeed, they offer an efficient solution for the automation of decision-making processes: mobility management, data transmission, etc. However, the use of such tools is necessarily associated with a significant additional cost: calculation, latency, etc. Therefore, it will be necessary to determine optimal tools to meet the requirements of the vehicular environment which may, in some emergency situations, require very low latency decision making processes. It will then be necessary to integrate these tools into the Blockchain framework. This is today a significant challenge for Blockchain networks [5].

4.2   An Optimal Positioning of the Blockchain Nodes

The proposed Blockchain architecture aims at enabling the deployment of Blockchain nodes at different levels (cf. Fig. 1): vehicles, UE network equipment, cloud servers. However, using all the available devices as Blockchain nodes would be meaningless. The higher the number of Blockchain nodes, the longer the consensus time will be. Such a solution would not be able to meet the requirements of C-ITS applications (latency, bandwidth). Moreover, it would lead to a useless over-consumption of energy (storage, calculation, communication). Therefore, it will be necessary to determine an optimal deployment of Blockchain nodes. This deployment will have to guarantee a high level of data availability. It will also have to take into account vehicles mobility and, thus, to enable the real-time activation/deactivation of Blockchain nodes and the migration of Blockchain data.

4.3   A Trade-Off Between the Different Requirements Identified

If we consider separately the different elements presented in Sect. 3 (vehicular context, applications requirements, users preferences, vehicle capabilities), the implementation of the Blockchain framework may seem simple. However, considering them together, its implementation seems much more complex. Indeed, some of these elements are opposed. Reinforcing the security level of C-ITS applications will necessarily imply a lower Quality of Service (cf. Sect. 3.3). Similarly, by distributing the load fairly among the different Blockchain nodes, the level of security or Quality of Service could be reduced (malicious nodes). Consequently, it will be necessary to define a priority order between these different elements. It will also be necessary to determine a trade-off between these different requirements. In specific situations (lack of infrastructure, low number of vehicles, etc.), reaching such a compromise may be complex.

4.4   The Definition of an Evaluation Environment

A final important challenge will be to define an evaluation/simulation/emulation environment that will enable us to demonstrate the performance level of the proposed Blockchain framework. In fact, at the moment, no tool is available to evaluate the performance of Blockchain architectures in a mobile environment. Beyond a challenge, the definition of such an evaluation environment could be an interesting starting point for numerous researchers working on the Blockchain technology in vehicular networks and, more broadly, mobile environments. The use of tools usually considered in the vehicular environment (OMNET, ns-2, ns3, Mininet-WiFi, SUMO, etc.) could be envisaged to design such an environment. Some possible guidelines are proposed in Sect. 3.2.

5   Conclusions

Distributed systems and, in particular, the Blockchain technology, appear today as an efficient way to reinforce security in the Internet of Vehicles and to establish trust between vehicles. However, the application of this technology in vehicular networks requires to take into account the specific features of this environment.

That is why, in this paper, we focus on the definition of a Blockchain framework adapted to the Internet of Vehicles. To do this, we first highlight the limitations of existing work. Thereafter, we identify four essential characteristics of the vehicular environment: the vehicular context (mobility, link lifetime, etc.), the variable requirements of vehicular applications (Quality of Service, security, etc.), the user preferences (privacy, etc.) and the variable capabilities of the vehicles (storage, computing, communication, etc.). We then propose an architecture and mechanisms that could take these different elements into account to define a Blockchain framework adapted to vehicular networks. Finally, we present future directions that will enable the implementation and evaluation of this framework.

References

1. Androulaki, E., et al.: Hyperledger fabric: a distributed operating system for permissioned blockchains. In: Proceedings of the Thirteenth EuroSys Conference, pp. 1–15 (2018)
2. Androulaki, E., Cachin, C., De Caro, A., Kokoris-Kogias, E.: Channels: horizontal scaling and confidentiality on permissioned blockchains. In: Lopez, J., Zhou, J., Soriano, M. (eds.) ESORICS 2018. LNCS, vol. 11098, pp. 111–131. Springer, Cham (2018). https://doi.org/10.1007/978-3-319-99073-6_6
3. Behrisch, M., Bieker, L., Erdmann, J., Krajzewicz, D.: Sumo simulation of urban mobility: an overview. In: Proceedings of SIMUL 2011, The Third International Conference on Advances in System Simulation, ThinkMind (2011)
4. Cordova, D., Laube, A., Pujolle, G., et al.: Blockgraph: a blockchain for mobile ad hoc networks. In: 2020 4th Cyber Security in Networking Conference (CSNet), pp. 1–8. IEEE (2020)
5. Dinh, T.N., Thai, M.T.: AI and blockchain: a disruptive integration. Computer 51(9), 48–53 (2018)
6. Festag, A.: Cooperative intelligent transport systems standards in Europe. IEEE Commun. Mag. 52(12), 166–172 (2014)
7. Fontes, R.R., Afzal, S., Brito, S.H., Santos, M.A., Rothenberg, C.E.: Mininet-wifi: emulating software-defined wireless networks. In: 2015 11th International Conference on Network and Service Management (CNSM), pp. 384–389. IEEE (2015)
8. Gómez-Gutiérrez, D., Vázquez, C.R., Čelikovský, S., Sánchez-Torres, J.D., Ruiz-León, J.: On finite-time and fixed-time consensus algorithms for dynamic networks switching among disconnected digraphs. Int. J. Control 93(9), 2120–2134 (2020)
9. Hu, Y., Lu, Q., Hu, Y.: Event-based communication and finite-time consensus control of mobile sensor networks for environmental monitoring. Sensors 18(8), 2547 (2018)
10. Hussain, R., Lee, J., Zeadally, S.: Trust in VANET: a survey of current solutions and future research opportunities. IEEE Trans. Intell. Transp. Syst. 22(5), 2553–2571 (2020)
11. Kang, J., Xiong, Z., Niyato, D., Ye, D., Kim, D.I., Zhao, J.: Toward secure blockchain-enabled internet of vehicles: optimizing consensus management using reputation and contract theory. IEEE Trans. Veh. Technol. 68(3), 2906–2920 (2019)
12. Kudva, S., Badsha, S., Sengupta, S., Khalil, I., Zomaya, A.: Towards secure and practical consensus for blockchain based VANET. Inf. Sci. 545, 170–187 (2021)

13. Liaskos, S., Wang, B., Alimohammadi, N.: Blockchain networks as adaptive systems. In: 2019 IEEE/ACM 14th International Symposium on Software Engineering for Adaptive and Self-Managing Systems (SEAMS), pp. 139–145. IEEE (2019)
14. Liu, M., Teng, Y., Yu, F.R., Leung, V.C., Song, M.: Deep reinforcement learning based performance optimization in blockchain-enabled internet of vehicle. In: ICC 2019–2019 IEEE International Conference on Communications (ICC), pp. 1–6. IEEE (2019)
15. Lu, Z., Liu, W., Wang, Q., Qu, G., Liu, Z.: A privacy-preserving trust model based on blockchain for VANETS. IEEE Access 6, 45655–45664 (2018)
16. Manvi, S.S., Tangade, S.: A survey on authentication schemes in VANETS for secured communication. Veh. Commun. 9, 19–30 (2017)
17. Mendiboure, L., Chalouf, M.A., Krief, F.: Towards a blockchain-based SD-ioV for applications authentication and trust management. In: Skulimowski, A.M.J., Sheng, Z., Khemiri-Kallel, S., Cérin, C., Hsu, C.-H. (eds.) IOV 2018. LNCS, vol. 11253, pp. 265–277. Springer, Cham (2018). https://doi.org/10.1007/978-3-030-05081-8_19
18. Mendiboure, L., Chalouf, M.A., Krief, F.: A scalable blockchain-based approach for authentication and access control in software defined vehicular networks. In: 2020 29th International Conference on Computer Communications and Networks (ICCCN), pp. 1–11. IEEE (2020)
19. Mendiboure, L., Chalouf, M.A., Krief, F.: Survey on blockchain-based applications in internet of vehicles. Computers & Electrical Engineering 84, 106646 (2020)
20. Mendiboure, L., Chalouf, M.A., Krief, F.: Toward new intelligent architectures for the internet of vehicles. In: Intelligent Network Management and Control: Intelligent Security, Multi-criteria Optimization, Cloud Computing, Internet of Vehicles, Intelligent Radio pp. 193–215 (2021)
21. Pilkington, M.: Blockchain technology: principles and applications. In: Research handbook on digital transformations. Edward Elgar Publishing, McCann (2016)
22. Rai, S., Hood, K., Nesterenko, M., Sharma, G.: Blockguard: Adaptive blockchain security. arXiv preprint arXiv:1907.13232 (2019)
23. Ravindran, R.: Circle of trust: a high volume, energy efficient, stake blind and high attack tolerant blockchain consensus protocol. In: 2019 IEEE 12th International Conference on Global Security, Safety and Sustainability (ICGS3), pp. 1–4. IEEE (2019)
24. Singh, M., Salam, I.: Adaptive proof of driving consensus for intelligent vehicle communication. In: Information Security of Intelligent Vehicles Communication. SCI, vol. 978, pp. 229–237. Springer, Singapore (2021). https://doi.org/10.1007/978-981-16-2217-5_15
25. Wu, J., Dong, M., Ota, K., Li, J., Yang, W.: Application-aware consensus management for software-defined intelligent blockchain in IoT. IEEE Netw. 34(1), 69–75 (2020)
26. Yang, F., Wang, S., Li, J., Liu, Z., Sun, Q.: An overview of internet of vehicles. China Commun. 11(10), 1–15 (2014)
27. Yang, Y.T., Chou, L.D., Tseng, C.W., Tseng, F.H., Liu, C.C.: Blockchain-based traffic event validation and trust verification for VANETS. IEEE Access 7, 30868–30877 (2019)
28. Yaqoob, I., Ahmad, I., Ahmed, E., Gani, A., Imran, M., Guizani, N.: Overcoming the key challenges to establishing vehicular communication: Is SDN the answer? IEEE Commun. Mag. 55(7), 128–134 (2017)

Traffic Light Priority in NordicWay

Felipe Valle[1]([✉])[iD], Alexey Vinel[1][iD], and Mikael Erneberg[2]

[1] Halmstad University, Halmstad, Sweden
{felipe.valle,alexey.vinel}@hh.se
[2] EVAM H&E Solutions AB, Stockholm, Sweden
mikael@evam.life

Abstract. In this work we introduce our efforts to implement a vehicular (V2X) communication system that is fully compliant with the requirements of the Scandinavian NordicWay project. In particular, we focus our efforts on the implementation of the project's Traffic Signal Priority use case in which selected vehicles are able to send signal request messages (SRMs) to the traffic light controller in order to request priority for green light at specific intersections. We discuss the basic flow of the request/response messages, how messages are constructed according to the geographic data of the road infrastructure. Finally, we show how a vehicle sends messages using the Interchange, the key component of the NordicWay project, and its distinctive characteristic versus other state of the art vehicular communication frameworks.

Keywords: VANET · C-ITS · Connected vehicles · Prototype

1 Introduction

Intelligent Transportation Systems (ITS) embrace a wide variety of communications related applications intended to increase travel safety, minimize environmental impact and improve traffic management. In Europe the most robust ITS development architecture is the ETSI C-ITS (Cooperative ITS) framework [1,2]. C-ITS is, at its core, a collection of technologies and standards that regulate the information exchange between road users and infrastructure. However, its deployment faces many important problems still unresolved, such as legal, organisational, administrative, governing aspects, technical and standardisation aspects as well as implementation and procurement issues.

In order to solve some of these issues, a joint initiative of European Member States and road operators for testing and implementing C-ITS services aiming to achieve cross-border harmonisation and interoperability was created. This is

The research leading to the results reported in this work has received funding from the Knowledge Foundation (KKS) in "Safety of Connected Intelligent Vehicles in Smart Cities – SafeSmart" project (2019–2023), Swedish Innovation Agency (VINNOVA) in "Emergency Vehicle Traffic Light Pre-emption in Cities – EPIC" project (2020–2022) and the ELLIIT Strategic Research Network.

© Springer Nature Switzerland AG 2021
J. Moreno García-Loygorri et al. (Eds.): Nets4Cars/Nets4Trains/Nets4Aircraft 2021, LNCS 13120, pp. 49–55, 2021.
https://doi.org/10.1007/978-3-030-92684-7_5

known as the *C-Roads Platform* [3,4]. Within the C-Roads framework, the setup and operation of the different test pilots is the responsibility of each member state, in Scandinavia in particular, the official C-Roads partner is the *NordicWay Project*. NordicWay is a C-ITS pilot project that enables vehicles, infrastructure and network operators to communicate safety hazards and other information from roads in the Nordic countries between different stakeholders. The current version of the pilot is NordicWay3 with the last activity report for the previous version being available since the end of the last year [8].

In this paper we introduce our implementation of a NordicWay standard compliant vehicular (V2X) communication system. This system will be used by emergency vehicles in order to request traffic light priority at signalized intersections by interacting with the specific region's traffic light controller (TLC) [6].

2   C-Roads/NordicWay Framework

2.1   C-ITS Communication

Usually, when we talk about vehicular networks (VANETs) we assume that the communication is either vehicle-to-vehicle (V2V) or vehicle-to-infrastructure (V2I). That is, vehicles send messages directly to other neighbouring vehicles or to road side units (RSUs) which relay messages to a larger area. This is what is normally referred to as ITS-G5. However, in the C-Roads framework, the users are also allowed to communicate directly with service providers using any communication technology of their choice (IP, WiFi, etc.). These service entities then interact with the rest of the network using a specific IP-based channel called the basic interface (BI) whose purpose is to provide interoperability between different applications and service providers.

2.2   Basic Interface

In C-Roads (and NordicWay), the BI is an IP-Based information sharing channel/protocol that allows interaction between C-ITS actors (and potential third parties). It is independent of any deployment model that Member States or C-ITS actors choose to deploy. The data is exchanged using the Advanced Message Queuing Protocol (AMQP) which provides basic transport level security (TLS) and also allows for the exchange of non C-ITS messages. Optionally, this exchange may involve the use of an intermediary message broker.

2.3   AMQP Protocol

Is an Application Layer protocol that focuses on process-to-process communication across IP networks. It enables client applications to communicate with messaging middleware brokers. Thus, it can be seen as an analogue to HTTP but for publisher/subscriber transactions instead of request/response. AMQP is also payload agnostic which allows different payload formats to be carried.

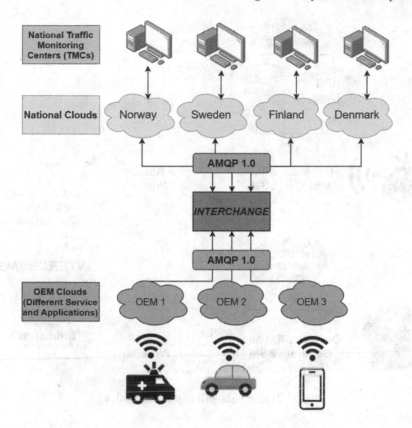

Fig. 1. NordicWay interchange architecture

2.4 NordicWay Interchange Node

The main goal of NordicWay is to establish a solution that allows for cross-border continuity and interoperability of the C-ITS use cases deployed in Finland, Sweden, Norway and Denmark. Thus, there was a need for a mechanism that could enable the information exchange between different service providers, and between service providers and the traffic data providers (e.g., in case the driver is driving abroad).

The mechanism agreed between the partners of the project was the use of an intermediary NordicWay server, which is a central hub that facilitates the interchange of messages of interest between countries, service clouds and traffic monitoring centers (TMCs). This server is referred to as the *Interchange* and the architectural model is shown in Fig. 1.

The architecture of the Interchange is based on the following two main requirements: It must allow inter-operable exchange and crowd sourcing of digital traffic information related to traffic safety like hazards, road works, etc.; and it must be lightweight, primarily capable of providing secure message routing between actors through standardized interfaces.

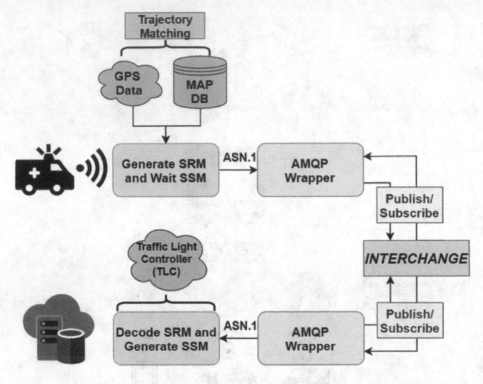

Fig. 2. Traffic light priority message flow

It is important to note that communication with the interchange works via a publisher and subscriber system (as seen in Fig. 2) in which users subscribe to specific message queues (also called topic exchanges) and the interchange acts as an AMQP message broker. This AMQP broker is based on protocol version 1.0 and is implemented (in the NordicWay2 version) using an Apache QPID server.

An important building block of the interchange is its Geo-lookup component, implemented using PostGis, this allows the delivery of messages to subscribers located in specific geographical areas (from a city to a single intersection) helping ensure that the information reaches only the affected vehicles (for example in case of a road accident or a malfunctioning traffic light) while also providing transport layer security across countries.

In summary, the *Interchange Application* performs the following functions: Reads and validates the AMQP messages written by the data producers; performs Geo-lookup of the valid messages and creates multiple copies of the same AMQP message depending on its results; finally, it pushes the messages to the different topic exchanges which are listened to by the subscribers.

3   Messaging System

3.1   SAE Messages

In order to implement the Traffic Signal Priority application compliant with the NordicWay specifications the system needs to be able to send and receive three specific message types: the Signal Request Message (SRM), the Signal Status Message (SSM) and MAP Messages. The specific format and content of these messages is specified in the SAE J2735 standard for vehicular messages [7].

The basic flow of the implemented messaging system (shown in Fig. 2) can be described as follows:

- First, an emergency vehicle equipped with our messaging interface is driving towards a signalized intersection. The vehicle is subscribed to the Interchange's MAP publishing application [8] and is able to receive periodic MAP messages containing the geometric information of the signalized road infrastructure.
- The Interchange is able to determine which specific MAP message a vehicle receives using the broker's Geo-lookup capabilities. Thus, a vehicle only receives the MAP message relevant to the signalized intersections it is approaching to.
- The vehicle decodes the MAP message and runs a trajectory matching algorithm in combination with its GPS route data in order to determine on which specific lane is going to arrive to the intersection.
- When the matching completes, the vehicle builds a SRM and sends it to the TLC through the interchange containing the required information (Intersection ID, Vehicle ID, Estimated Time of Arrival (ETA), Approach Lane, etc.). Then, the interchange ensures message delivery to the correct TLC.
- SAE J2735 messages are encoded using the ASN.1 interface description language with Basic Packed Encoding Rules (PER) and thus must be first wrapped around an AMQP message before sending to the Interchange.
- The vehicle then waits and periodically receives SSMs containing the status of the request response (e.g. processing, accepted, rejected, etc.) and then adapts accordingly.
- It is important to note that the SSMs sent from the TLC also go through the same process of ANS.1 encoding and AMQP wrapping but the publisher/subscriber roles are swapped between the TLC and the emergency vehicle for this exchange.
- If the ETA to an intersection changes during the traffic maneuver, the SRM must be updated and resent to the TLC in order to keep it as active, otherwise, the request will expire before crossing the intersection.

The NordicWay project partners require that emergency vehicles using the traffic signal priority service send their SRMs in bunches (generating them from a list of intersections along their routes) in order to packet them together and generate what is know as a *green wave* in which the intersections along the route are sequentially turned green as the vehicle advances making the system operation more efficient.

Fig. 3. California test bed intersection map

3.2   Preliminary Results

Since there is no MAP data readily available from the Swedish NordicWay Pilot yet, we decided to use data from the California Connected Vehicles TestBed [5]. Then, we built a simulated version of the Interchange using the same Apache QPID technology in which the NordicWay2 Interchange version is based on [8].

We were able to simulate a sample trajectory for an emergency vehicle using real time GPS data obtained from the Mapbox SDK (Fig. 4) traveling back and forth through three real intersections (see Fig. 3) while requesting traffic signal priority via the Interchange. The average trip time between these intersections ranges from 5 to 10 min depending on traffic conditions.

We also simulated the TLC side of the communication by sending SSMs with different responses to the requesting vehicle in order to test the messaging system encoding and decoding of SAE messages. The results are extremely promising, the system is able to decode geographic data from MAP messages and generate adequate SRMs on-demand using trajectory matching with real time navigation data. By using an adequate MAP database it is also possible to generate a *green wave* using trajectory matching on a sequence of consecutive intersections.

Simulations show that providing the emergency vehicle with green phase at signalized intersections reduces average trip time by approximately 20% whilst

Fig. 4. Test trajectory GPS data

increasing traffic safety by reducing the risk of collisions. Finally, the emergency vehicle can adjust its trajectory according to the received SSM status responses received from the TLC, while simultaneously, it can also update the TLC on unexpected trajectory changes by sending new SRM requests, updates or cancellations as needed.

References

1. ETSI EN 302 665 Intelligent Transport Systems (ITS); Communications Architecture. ETSI, Sophia Antipolis Cedex, France (2010)
2. ETSI TR 101 607 Intelligent Transport Systems (ITS); Cooperative ITS (C-ITS); Release 1. ETSI, Sophia Antipolis Cedex, France (2020)
3. Böhm, M.: C-Roads-The Platform of Harmonised C-ITS Deployment in Europe (2016)
4. Böhm, M., Platform, S.G.C.R.: C-roads-deployment of C-ITS services throughout Europe. In: Proceedings of the 1st EU-ASEAN Workshop on Intelligent Transport Systems (ITS), Singapore (2019)
5. Caltrans: California Department of Transportation: California Connected Vehicles Testbed (2019). http://caconnectedvehicletestbed.org/index.php/index.php
6. da Costa, L.A.L.F., Duarte, E.K., Erneberg, M., de Freitas, E.P., Vinel, A.: Poster: safesmart - a VANET system for efficient communication for emergency vehicles. In: 2020 IFIP Networking Conference (2020)
7. International, S.: Dedicated Short Range Communications (DSRC) Message Set Dictionary. SAE J2735 (2016)
8. NordicWay2: Final report - Activity 9 Swedish Pilot (2020)

Nets4Trains

Radio Resource Management in Next-Generation Railway System with Heterogeneous Multi-hop Relaying Deployment

Qianrui Li[✉], Akl Charaf, Nicolas Gresset, and Hervé Bonneville

Mitsubishi Electric R&D Centre Europe (MERCE), Rennes, France
{q.li,a.charaf,n.gresset,h.bonneville}@fr.merce.mee.com

Abstract. Heterogeneous multi-hop relaying deployment that involves both Uu and PC5 interface is potentially a promising technology to overcome the high propagation loss, blockage and mobility sensitivity in millimeter wave band communication for next-generation railway system. In this context, we analyze the radio resource management that targets different train applications under such deployment. Adopting the system deployment, channel and antenna configuration of 3GPP, we propose an approach that jointly optimizes radio resource management and routing topology for multi-hop relaying transmission involving both Uu and PC5 interface. The system level simulation results exhibit that the joint optimization outperforms the existing conventional algorithm. Simulations and analysis can also serve as feasibility analysis and guideline for a possible architecture in future train radio deployment.

Keywords: Multi-hop relaying · Sidelink PC5 · Millimeter wave train radio · Radio resource management

1 Introduction

The future of intelligent transport system involves a modal shift of human-controlled functionality toward the full automation paradigm by virtue of new communication technologies. For next-generation railway communication system, millimeter wave (mmWave) band train radio communication is identified as a promising technology to solve the spectrum scarcity problem in train communication domain. It is recognized as a key enabler toward greener, smarter and more robust intelligent transport system. International railway union (UIC) has launched the Future Railway Mobile Communication System (FRMCS) project, with the support of the European Union Agency for Railways (EURA), in which railway operators specify the requirements of a next generation train standard. In July 2015, a new European Telecommunications Standards Institute (ETSI)

This work was performed in the framework of ANR mmW4Rail project, Grant ANR-20-CE22-0011-03.

© Springer Nature Switzerland AG 2021
J. Moreno García-Loygorri et al. (Eds.): Nets4Cars/Nets4Trains/Nets4Aircraft 2021, LNCS 13120, pp. 59–70, 2021.
https://doi.org/10.1007/978-3-030-92684-7_6

group was launched as ETSI Technical Committee on Railway Telecommunications (ETSI TC-RT). Shift2Rail aims also at participating to the evolution of the future train communication system. In the meantime, the investigation on next generation cellular communication systems is at its height and high speed train scenario has been particularly identified in 3GPP so as to target consistent passenger user experience and critical train communication reliability with very high mobility [1,2].

In mmWave band, severe attenuation of signals caused by path loss and attenuation in mmWave band render distinct deployment from conventional sub-6 GHz train radio systems. Therefore, multi-hop relaying based on radio units close to the rail track is a promising technology which involves using spatially dispersed nodes as well as transmission between such nodes in shorter range so as to compensate the high propagation loss, blockage and mobility sensitivity in mmWave communication [3].

Multi-hop relay channel and networks have already been extensively studied in the literature [4–12]. Theoretical analysis on the decode-and-forward relaying and amplify-and-forward relay channel have been conducted in [4,5]. Different optimization metrics in a multi-hop relaying network such as optimal routing path selection [6,12], end-to-end delay [6,7], secrecy [8], throughput [6,8] and fairness [9] as well as combinations of such metrics have been considered. In this work, we focus on a heterogeneous multi-hop relaying deployment which highlights complementarity between cellular long-range technologies using the Uu interface and short-range sidelink (SL) technologies using PC5 interface.

In this work, we target arbitrary train radio communication applications which can be either passenger-oriented business applications, or safety-related performance and critical applications [13]. Those applications vary from passenger information system and/or recreational services such as on-board video streaming, games and real-time news delivery to Close Circuit Television (CCTV) communication service for surveillance cameras, train coupling, voice communication for operational purposes and communication based train control. Those services generally target either stringent delay or throughput constraints. Therefore, a throughput/delay-aware optimization is crucial. Due to the shorter coverage offered by mmW radio, we consider an heterogeneous deployment scenario, mixing macro cells and multi-hop relaying. Under such an heterogeneous multi-hop relaying deployment, we propose a joint radio resource management and routing topology management aiming at a predefined throughput/delay metric for multiple trains. Our main contributions are twofold:

- A theoretical analysis that formulates the delay or throughput performance aware joint radio resource management and routing topology management for multi-users multi-hop transmission problem into a mixed discrete-continuous optimization problem.
- System level simulation results which confirm that the proposed algorithm outperforms conventional strategy. They can serve as feasibility analysis to justify the heterogeneous multi-hop relaying deployment in next-generation railway communication system.

2   Problem Description

2.1   Heterogeneous Multi-hop Relaying Deployment

The heterogeneous multi-hop relaying deployment is illustrated in Fig. 1. It is coherent with the high speed train deployment in 3GPP which focuses on the train communication reliability with very high mobility [1,14]. It is also coherent with one of the technical approaches identified by 5GAA for Cooperative Intelligent Transport Systems (C-ITS) services [15]. For train applications which involve communication between the 5G gNB and the train, we consider that apart from the conventional cellular deployment of 5G gNBs, there exists multiple network devices called Road Side Units (RSUs) located along both sides of rail tracks for train communication. The RSUs can communicate with 5G gNB. This communication is based on conventional long-range uplink/downlink (UL/DL) Uu interface. In addition, the RSUs can also communicate with trains and adjacent RSUs. This is supported by short-range device-to-device technologies using for example 3GPP SL PC5 interfaces. Therefore, depending on radio resource management and routing topology management, messages can be delivered from gNB via RSU(s) to trains with multi-hop communication.

This deployment is particularly interesting for train-to-infrastructure (T2I) services because such deployment which entails a mixture of cellular network infrastructure and additional support via RSU-based infrastructure can accommodate both delay tolerant and low latency services [15]. In addition, RSU-based infrastructure also renders better coverage, stronger signal reception and more dynamic radio resource and routing topology management.

2.2   Radio Resource Management for UL/DL and SL

According to Sect. 2.1, both UL/DL and SL communication could be involved in the transmission between gNB and train. For the UL/DL communication, Uu interface is used. In 5G NR, the UL/DL scheduling can be based on dynamic grant for aperiodic traffic scheduling or without dynamic grant for periodic traffic scheduling.

For DL dynamic scheduling, each scheduled UE is provided with scheduling assignment. The scheduling assignment is transmitted just before the data on the Physical Downlink Shared Channel (PDSCH) and includes information on the set of time-frequency resources upon which the device's DL shared channel is transmitted [16]. For UL dynamic scheduling, UE without a valid scheduling grant can send a scheduling request on the Physical Uplink Control Channel (PUCCH) to ask the network for a UL scheduling grant. The gNB will send the grant on the Physical Downlink Control Channel (PDCCH). This UL scheduling grant indicates the set of time/frequency/spatial resources to use for the UL shared channel as well as the associated transport format [16]. For DL scheduling without dynamic grant, semi-persistent scheduling is supported where the device is configured with a periodicity of the data transmissions using RRC signaling. For UL scheduling without dynamic grant, configured grants which provide

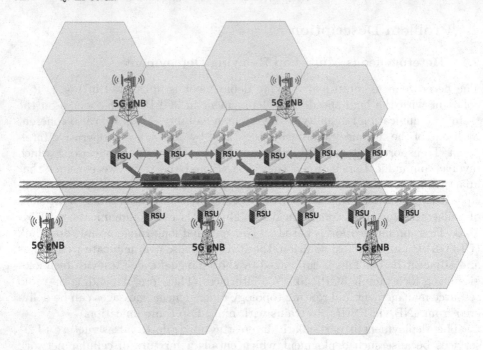

Fig. 1. Heterogeneous multi-hop relaying from gNB via RSUs to trains.

periodical grants for UL transmission can be used [16]. The differences between semi-persistent scheduling and configured grant scheduling are based on how the transmissions are activated/deactivated and how the transmission configuration is signaled. For semi-persistent scheduling, the configuration of periodicity is based on RRC signaling and the activation of semi-persistent scheduling is done using the PDCCH with the CS-RNTI. For UL configured grant scheduling, the configuration is based on RRC signaling. However, the activation/deactivation of transmission can either based on RRC signaling or L1/L2 control signaling similar to the DL semi-persistent scheduling, depending on which type of Configured grant is used [16].

For the SL communication, PC5 interface is used. In 5G NR V2X, there are two modes (mode 1 and 2) for SL resource selection. In mode 1, UEs are in the network coverage. 5G gNB will use NR Uu interface to perform SL radio resource management. In mode 1, SL scheduling can be based on either dynamic grant or configured grant. With dynamic grant, UE will send a scheduling request to the gNB using the PUCCH. The gNB will respond with the Downlink Control Information (DCI) over the PDCCH. The SL resources allocated for the SL transmission are indicated in the DCI. With configured grant, the gNB can assign a set of pre-allocated SL resources to a UE for transmitting periodic traffic [17]. In mode 2, UEs can operate without network coverage, which means UEs will perform the SL radio resource management in autonomous manner. In mode 2, SL scheduling can be based on either dynamic grant or semi-persistent scheduling. The dynamic grant scheduling and semi-persistent scheduling in mode 2 are very similar regarding the SL resource selection. The only difference result from the fact that the dynamic scheme only selects resources for a Transport Block (TB) while the semi-persistent scheme selects resources for several TBs [17]. Table 1 summarizes the scheduling schemes for DL, UL and SL communication in 5G NR.

Table 1. Scheduling schemes for DL, UL and SL communication in 5G NR.

Link type		Aperiodic traffic	Periodic traffic
DL		Dynamic scheduling with scheduling assignment	Semi-persistent scheduling
UL		Dynamic scheduling with scheduling request and scheduling grant	Configured grant scheduling
SL	Mode 1	Dynamic grant scheduling	Configured grant scheduling
	Mode 2	Dynamic grant scheduling	Semi-persistent scheduling

In this paper, we assume that the traffic is aperiodic and dynamic scheduling is used for UL/DL and SL communication. For SL, we assume that NR V2X mode 1 is applied. For the sake of simplicity, from now on we only consider DL transmission from gNB to trains potentially via multi-hop relaying, UL transmission can be analyzed in similar manner. With those assumptions, according to Sect. 2.2, gNB is responsible for the DL and SL resource management. There is in general little discrepancy between SL and DL physical layer resource configurations. SL radio resources can be allocated from licensed carriers dedicated to SL communications or from licensed carriers that share resources between SL and UL communications [17]. However, there is one important difference between the DL/UL and SL resources which imposes specific constraint for the scheduling. In NR V2X, a subset of the available SL resources is (pre-)configured to be used by several UEs for their SL transmissions. This indicates that the SL resource pool is shared among several UEs potentially served by different gNBs, while for the DL resources each gNB manages its own resource pool.

In this paper, we further assume that there are simultaneous communication between gNB and several trains through multi-hop transmissions. Each train may or may not have the same application for their individual communication, but all those UEs share the same SL resource pool for the SL communication in the multi-hop relaying. We assume that both DL and SL resource sharing are performed in Time Division Multi-Access (TDMA) manner. This implies that all Uu links pertaining to the same gNB will share their resource allocation in time domain, and all PC5 links (i.e., RSU-to-train, RSU-to-RSU) for all UEs' multi-hop relaying will share their resource allocation in time domain on a unique SL resource pool.

Thus, the problem of radio resource management with heterogeneous multi-hop relaying deployment becomes a joint optimization of (i) multi-hop relaying topology between gNB and multiple trains, and (ii) TDMA resource allocation strategies for involved Uu and PC5 links in each gNB's Uu link resource pool and the unique PC5 link resource pool. Depending on the targeted service/application at each train, the utility function for optimization can be a throughput related metric or a delay related metric.

3 System Model

We consider a heterogeneous multi-hop relaying deployment including M gNBs, N RSUs and K trains. The muti-hop routing topology of an arbitrary train k can be denoted as $\pi^{(k)}$, where $\pi^{(k)} = (\pi_1^{(k)}, \pi_2^{(k)}, \ldots, \pi_{L_k}^{(k)})$. The total number of hops is L_k and $\pi_\ell^{(k)}$ indicates the ℓ-th hop for the multi-hop relaying. For the hop $\pi_\ell^{(k)}$, it can be further denoted by a pair of vertices (V_i, V_j) for this hop. For the heterogeneous multi-hop relaying deployment considered in this paper, the first hop $\pi_1^{(k)} = (V_{\text{gNB}_m}, V_{\text{RSU}_n})$ is always a Uu link between an arbitrary gNB m and an arbitrary first selected RSU n. The successive hops $\pi_{2,\ldots,L_{k-1}}^{(k)} = (V_{\text{RSU}_i}, V_{\text{RSU}_j})$ are PC5 links between RSUs. It should be noticed that $\pi_\ell^{(k)}(2) = \pi_{\ell+1}^{(k)}(1)$, which ensures that the multi-hop routing path is a connected graph. The last hop $\pi_{L_k}^{(k)} = (V_{\text{RSU}_j}, V_{\text{Train}_k})$ is a PC5 link between RSU and train.

As presented earlier, we consider a TDMA resource sharing for the Uu link and PC5 link resources. Let $t_{\pi_\ell^{(k)}}$ denote the fraction of resource in time domain that has been allocated for transmitting hop $\pi_\ell^{(k)}$. According to Sect. 2.2, all Uu links pertaining to the same gNB will share their resource allocation in time domain. This will lead to a per-gNB resource allocation constraint:

$$\sum_{k=1}^{K} \mathbb{1}_{\pi_1^{(k)}(1)=V_{\text{gNB}_m}} \cdot t_{\pi_1^{(k)}} = 1, \forall m = 1, \ldots, M.$$

The expression $\mathbb{1}_{\pi_1^{(k)}(1)=V_{\text{gNB}_m}}$ is an indicator function which returns 1 if the first vertex of the first hop $\pi_1^{(k)}$ is the gNB m, otherwise 0 is returned.

Regarding all PC5 links, since there is a unique SL resource pool, the constraint reads:

$$\sum_{k=1}^{K}\sum_{\ell=2}^{L_k} t_{\pi_\ell^{(k)}} = 1.$$

4 Joint Radio Resource Management and Routing Topology Optimization

In this section, we formulate the routing path selection and TDMA resource sharing decision for both Uu and PC5 resource pools into a joint optimization problem. The first step toward such goal is to properly define an utility function for optimization. As is mentioned before, the utility function can be a metric either related to throughput or delay, depending on the targeted application at each train.

4.1 Throughput-Aware Joint Optimization

Consider that the targeted applications are passenger-oriented business applications such as passenger information system and/or recreational services including board video streaming, games and real-time news delivery. The design criterion is to provide consistent user experience and maintain a stable link with good data-rate. In this case, throughput related metric should be applied.

Let $R_{\pi_\ell^{(k)}}$ denote the link capacity of the ℓ-th hop $\pi_\ell^{(k)}$ for train k. In the heterogeneous multi-hop relaying deployment, the end-to-end throughput is upper bounded by the hop with smallest throughput. Since we have simultaneous multiple trains transmission, the utility function should leverage among all the trains for a more fair radio resource management. Thus, criteria such as α-fair [18] or max-min user-fairness could be used. For ease of explanation, we consider hereby a max-min fair utility function so as to maximize the minimal end-to-end throughput among the K trains. Therefore, the throughput-aware joint optimization reads:

$$\max_{\{\pi_i^{(k)}, t_{\pi_i^{(k)}}\}} \quad \min_k \min_i t_{\pi_i^{(k)}} \cdot R_{\pi_i^{(k)}}$$

$$\text{s.t.} \quad \begin{aligned} &\sum_{k=1}^{K} \mathbb{1}_{\pi_1^{(k)}(1) = V_{\text{gNB}_m}} \cdot t_{\pi_1^{(k)}} = 1, \forall m = 1, \ldots, M \\ &\sum_{k=1}^{K} \sum_{\ell=2}^{L_k} t_{\pi_\ell^{(k)}} = 1 \\ &\pi^{(k)} = \left(\pi_1^{(k)}, \ldots, \pi_{L_k}^{(k)}\right) \in \Pi^{(k)} \\ &i = 1, \ldots, L_k \\ &k = 1, \ldots, K, \end{aligned} \qquad \text{(P1)}$$

where $\Pi^{(k)}$ is the set of all possible multi-hop routing topologies from gNB to train k.

The optimization problem (P1) is a mixed discrete-continuous multi-objective linear optimization problem. It should be noticed that if the routing topologies $\pi^{(k)}, \forall k$ are fixed, the aforementioned optimization over the TDMA resources $t_{\pi_i^{(k)}}, \forall k, \forall i$ can be reformulated into a linear programming by introducing a slack variable. Therefore, if the cardinality of $\Pi^{(k)}$ is not very big, a full search method can be applied by going through all possible combination of routing and solving each time the TDMA resources allocation linear programming. When the cardinality of $\Pi^{(k)}$ grows or the train number K increases, the number of all possible combination of routing becomes combinatorial, conventional method such as alternative optimization combined with branch-and-bound can be used to reduce the problem dimension and achieve sub-optimality.

4.2   Delay-Aware Joint Optimization

Assume the applications involved in this multi-hop relaying transmission are safety-related performance and critical applications such as CCTV communication service for surveillance cameras or train coupling. Those applications are characterized by stringent transmission latency. In this case, transmission delay related metric should be applied.

A realistic estimation of transmission delay includes multiple components such as transmission delay for the physical layer data plan transmission, channel access delay for associated physical layer control plan procedure, queueing delay in the Medium Access Control (MAC) layer and processing delay from upper layer. In this paper, solely physical layer data plan transmission delay is calculated as the delay metric for the optimization.

Let P_k denote the traffic for application at train k. Adopting the same notation for the link capacity $R_{\pi_\ell^{(k)}}$ and TDMA sharing strategy $t_{\pi_\ell^{(k)}}$ for the ℓ-th hop $\pi_\ell^{(k)}$ at train k, the transmission delay $T_{\pi_\ell^{(k)}}$ satisfies $T_{\pi_\ell^{(k)}} = \frac{P_k}{t_{\pi_\ell^{(k)}} \cdot R_{\pi_\ell^{(k)}} \cdot B_{\pi_\ell^{(k)}}}$, where $B_{\pi_\ell^{(k)}}$ denotes the bandwidth for the hop $\pi_\ell^{(k)}$. In the heterogeneous multi-hop relaying deployment, the end-to-end delay is the sum of per-hop transmission delay. Similar to the throughput-aware optimization, for ease of explanation, we consider hereby a min-max fair utility function so as to minimize the maximal end-to-end delay among the K trains. Therefore, the delay-aware joint optimization can be denoted as:

$$\min_{\{\pi_i^{(k)}, t_{\pi_i^{(k)}}\}} \max_k \sum_i \frac{P_k}{t_{\pi_i^{(k)}} \cdot R_{\pi_i^{(k)}} \cdot B_{\pi_i^{(k)}}}$$

$$\text{s.t.} \quad \begin{aligned} &\sum_{k=1}^{K} \mathbb{1}_{\pi_1^{(k)}(1)=V_{\mathrm{gNB}_m}} \cdot t_{\pi_1^{(k)}} = 1, \forall m = 1,\ldots,M \\ &\sum_{k=1}^{K} \sum_{\ell=2}^{L_k} t_{\pi_\ell^{(k)}} = 1 \\ &\pi^{(k)} = \left(\pi_1^{(k)},\ldots,\pi_{L_k}^{(k)}\right) \in \Pi^{(k)} \\ &i = 1,\ldots,L_k \\ &k = 1,\ldots,K. \end{aligned} \qquad \text{(P2)}$$

The optimization problem (P2) is a mixed discrete-continuous multi-objective nonlinear optimization problem. Conventional algorithms such as interior-point method, sequential quadratic programming or genetic algorithm can be used.

5   Simulation Results

In this section, we provide simulation results for the joint radio resource management and routing topology optimization under heterogeneous multi-hop relaying deployment. Simulations are performed on the 3GPP 5G NR compatible system level simulator developed in MERCE. As is shown in Fig. 1, heterogeneous multi-hop relaying deployment has two layers: a cellular deployment layer of 3-sectored gNBs as in [19] and a linear deployment layer [1] of RSUs with omni-directional single antenna. The channels for gNB to RSU, RSU to RSU and RSU to train links are based on the Rural enhanced Mobile Broad Band (Rural eMBB) channel model in [20].

Some deployment parameters are listed in Table 2. The parameters f_c Uu (PC5) and B Uu (PC5) represent the operating frequency and bandwidth of the Uu (PC5) links, respectively.

Table 2. Parameters for heterogeneous multi-hop relaying deployment in system level simulation.

M	N	K	f_c(Uu)	B(Uu)	f_c(PC5)	B(PC5)
19	15	4	2 GHz	5 MHz	30 GHz	80 MHz

In the simulations, we assume that each RSU can communicate to the gNB with either the strongest or the second strongest receiving power. We further assume that each of the 4 trains can communicate to the RSU with either the strongest or the second strongest receiving power. Thus, for each train, there are 4 possible routing topologies and there will be 256 combination of routing topologies for the 4 trains. During the Mont-Carlo simulation, each time 4 trains are randomly dropped. According to their positions, the corresponding Uu and PC5 links capacity $R_{\pi_i(k)}$ can be obtained in the system level simulator and corresponding joint optimization described in (P1) and (P2) are performed. In simulations of delay-aware optimization for applications with stringent latency requirements, we assume an application payload of $P_k = 800$ bits.

Figure 2 reveals that the proposed throughput-aware optimization outperforms the reference conventional algorithm, where the routing is only based on links with the strongest receiving power. A remarkable 50% increasing in the spectrum efficiency of end-to-end multi-hop transmission for half of the cases is observed in the cdf curve.

In Fig. 3, it can be concluded that the proposed delay-aware optimization outperforms the reference conventional algorithm, where the routing is only based on links with the strongest receiving power. For half of the cases, we observe around 20% decrease of end-to-end multi-hop transmission delay.

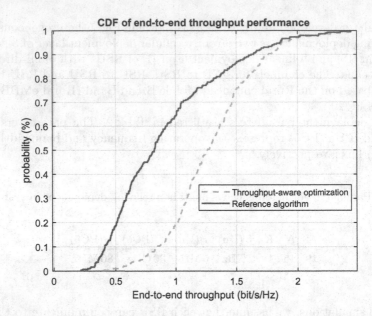

Fig. 2. CDF of end-to-end throughput performance under heterogeneous multi-hop relaying deployment.

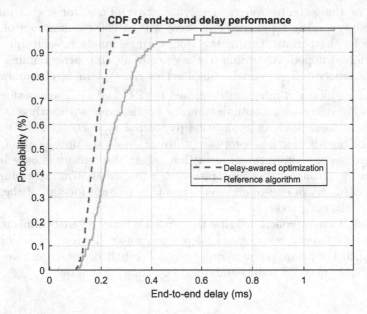

Fig. 3. CDF of end-to-end delay performance under heterogeneous multi-hop relaying deployment.

6 Conclusion

In this paper, we analyzed the heterogeneous multi-hop relaying for mmWave band train radio which targets both throughput and delay aware applications. A joint radio resource management and routing topology optimization is proposed to either maximize the minimal end-to-end throughput or minimize the maximal end-to-end transmission delay for multi-hop transmissions with several trains. The system level simulation results confirm that the proposed method outperforms the conventional algorithm. The study can also serve as a feasibility analysis for a potentially promising deployment architecture for next generation train radio.

References

1. TR38.913: Study on scenarios and requirements for next generation access technologies. Technical Specification Group Radio Access Network, 3rd Generation Partnership Project (3GPP), Tech. Rep., June 2018
2. Hasegawa, F., et al.: 3GPP standardization activities in relay based 5G high speed train scenarios for the SHF band. In: Proceedings Conference on Standards for Communications and Networking (CSCN) (2017)
3. Singh, S., Ziliotto, F., Madhow, U., Belding, E., Rodwell, M.: Blockage and directivity in 60 GHz wireless personal area networks: from cross-layer model to multi hop MAC design. IEEE J. Sel. Areas Commun. **27**(8), 1400–1413 (2009)
4. Gunduz, D., Khojastepour, M.A., Goldsmith, A., Poor, H.V.: Multi-hop MMO relay networks: diversity-multiplexing trade-off analysis. IEEE Trans. Wireless Commun. **9**(5), 1738–1747 (2010)
5. Ngo, H.Q., Larsson, E.G.: Linear multihop amplify-and-forward relay channels: error exponent and optimal number of hops. IEEE Trans. Wireless Commun. **10**(11), 3834–3842 (2011)
6. Vu, T.K., Liu, C.-F., Bennis, M., Debbah, M., Latva-Aho, M. : Path selection and rate allocation in self-backhauled mmWave networks. In: Proceedings of the IEEE Wireless Communications and Networking Conference (WCNC) (2018)
7. Hu, D., Wu, J., Fan, P.: Minimizing end-to-end delays in linear Multihop networks. IEEE Trans. Veh. Technol. **65**(8), 6487–6496 (2015)
8. Yao, J., Zhou, X., Liu, Y., Feng, S.: Secure transmission in linear Multihop relaying networks. IEEE Trans. Wireless Commun. **17**(2), 822–834 (2017)
9. Abuzainab, N., Touati, C.: Multihop relaying in millimeter wave networks: a proportionally fair cooperative network formation game. In: Proceedings of the IEEE Vehicular Technology Conference (VTC2015-Fall) (2015)
10. Scott, S., Leinonen, J., Pirinen, P., Vihriala, J., Van Phan, V., Latva-aho, M.: A cooperative moving relay node system deployment in a high speed train. In: Proceedings of the IEEE Vehicular Technology Conference (VTC Spring) (2013)
11. Sánchez, J.D.O., Alonso, J.I.: A two-hop MIMO relay architecture using LTE and millimeter wave bands in high-speed trains. IEEE Trans. Veh. Technol. **68**(3), 2052–2065 (2018)
12. Li, Q., Gresset, N.: Multi-hop relaying in mmWave band for next generation train radio. In: Proceeding of the. IEEE Vehicular Technology Conference (VTC2020-Spring) (2020)

13. FRMCS Traffic Analysis V2. UIC FRMCS for ECC FM56, Tech. Rep., September 2018
14. TR38.802: Study on scenarios and requirements for new radio access technology physical layer aspects. Technical Specification Group Radio Access Network, 3rd Generation Partnership Project (3GPP), Tech. Rep., September 2017
15. C-ITS Vehicle to infrastructure services: how C-V2X technology completely changes the cost equation for road operators. 5GAA, Tech. Rep., January 2019
16. Dahlman, E., Parkvall, S., Skold, J.: 5G NR: The Next Generation Wireless Access Technology. Academic Press, London (2020)
17. Garcia, M.H.C., et al.: A Tutorial on 5G NR V2X Communications. IEEE Commun. Surv. Tutor. **23**, 1972 –2026 (2021)
18. Altman, E., Avrachenkov, K., Garnaev, A.: Generalized α-fair resource allocation in wireless networks. In: Proceedings of the IEEE Conference on Decision and Control (CDC2008) (2008)
19. TR38.801: Study on new radio access technology: Radio access architecture and interfaces. Technical Specification Group Radio Access Network, 3rd Generation Partnership Project (3GPP), Tech. Rep., April 2017
20. Study on channel model for frequencies from 0.5 to 100 GHz (Release 14). Technical Specification Group Radio Access Network, 3rd Generation Partnership Project (3GPP), Tech. Rep., March 2017

Train-to-Train Connectivity
for Safety-Critical Use Cases

Cristian García Ruiz⬦, Juan Moreno García-Loygorri(✉)⬦,
and Berta Mazuecos Velázquez

Departamento de Ingeniería Audiovisual y Comunicaciones,
ETSIST UPM, Madrid, Spain
`juan.moreno.garcia-loygorri@upm.es`

Abstract. This paper develops some applications in which train-to-train (T2T) communications provide added value features to current railway communications systems, which are mainly based in train-to-ground (T2G) links. A campaign of measurements carried out in a Metro de Madrid depot is presented, where the feasibility of such systems is analyzed. The obtained results are both the jitter and delay in different situations. Besides, the broadcast of video over such link is tested.

Keywords: Train-to-train · Railway communications · Measurements · Safety-critical · Propagation

1   Introduction

Communications in railway environments are of great importance, mostly for safety matters, among other applications of interest. Basic safety in railways initially relied only on the train driver's quick reaction to the state of the lights that accounted for the occupancy state of the block ahead. With the evolution of communications, they were used to communicate the state of such signals to the train equipment on-board and then apply emergency braking in case the driver did not act properly to a restrictive state of the signal. Firstly, this communication was enabled by balises, empowered by either changes in magnetic fields or the use of radiofrequency signals, both received by on-board antennas placed at the bottom part of the trains.

However, this punctual information that takes part in the points where balises are deployed has been replaced with continuous information in order to increase the degree of protection of the trains, where each one is constantly receiving information. This is achieved mainly by both transmission through the rails and, most recently, via radiofrequency [2]. Radio in railway systems enables, for instance, the use of european rail traffic management system (ERTMS) over global system for mobile communications for railways (GSM-R), which is a special version of global system for mobile communications (GSM) devoted for railways. For metropolitan railways, the communications based train control (CBTC) systems that are being widely implemented since 2008, make use of the so-called WiFi bands.

Although these systems and their respective versions are the *de facto* standards in the railway industry for their features compared to their predecessors, they still rely on the communication via T2G links. Following this point, while still making use of the radio, the next step is to incorporate T2T links in railway communications environments. This new conception can enable both improvements on current systems and new use cases not even imagined yet.

In the literature, we can find, for example, some proposals on the addition of T2T links in a CBTC system architecture. In [9,15] trains are equipped with on-board zone controllers (ZCs). In [15] each consist derives its own movement authority (MA) based on the time of arrival (TOA) and sends it directly to other trains without the need of the interaction of the wayside equipment. However, for safety reasons, the wayside equipment can not be removed, but the whole architecture can be rethought. In [17] CBTC is proposed to be implemented through both direct links and relays that can overcome distances of several kilometers between the trains, while in [18] the long term evolution (LTE) version for vehicle to anything (V2X) is used for the direct communication links between the consists.

In order to test the feasibility of establishing T2T links, many tests have been carried out. In [8,16] a measurement campaign in an Italian high speed train (HST) line is analyzed, with trains running in parallel and in opposite directions. In [4] a measurement campaign in a subway tunnel at 900/2400 MHz is carried out, with different types of tunnels and train locations. In [5] ray-tracing (RT) simulations are used to derive the behaviour of T2T links in the THz band. On the other hand, in [7] a car is used to simulate the behaviour of a train even in a train crash. Different measurements for coupling and uncoupling situations at millimeter waves (mmWave) bands are analyzed in [14,20]. Finally, in [19] they obtain some results and highlights the effects of antenna misalignment.

Besides the safety improvements that T2T links could enable for railway systems and above exposed, more future use cases for these links are presented in Sect. 2.

In this work, a measurement campaign at mmWave bands is presented in Sect. 3. It is carried out at Metro de Madrid facilities with two trains in different situations that have been considered of interest. From this campaign, some results are extracted and analyzed to check the feasibility of the usage of the radios gently supplied by Radwin and take the first steps to build a real-world demonstrator.

Finally, a series of conclusions are raised in Sect. 5.

2   Use Cases

In this section, a series of use cases for T2T links are presented. The basic differences between T2T and T2G links are depicted in Fig. 1. For its direct communication between transmitter and receiver, the use of T2T links can be

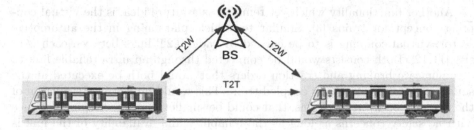

Fig. 1. Example of a T2T architecture [10].

mainly intended for applications where low latency is mandatory. It is noteworthy that latency implies more uncertainty about the data which means larger safety margins (and less efficiency).

As it has been highlighted in Sect. 1, communication systems for railways are mainly devoted to provide high standards of safety. Within this framework we could find, as already explained, the inclusion of T2T links in CBTC systems. For reliability and safety reasons, these links would not be intended to entirely replace the T2G links and eliminate all the wayside equipment, but gain new functionalities or increase the overall capacity of the communications system.

These direct connections between trains operating with CBTC systems could be used, for instance, to exchange their MAs point to point, leading to a substantial decrease of the end-to-end communication delays. Then, it could represent a significant reduction of the safety distance between trains [11,15,17]. This can be easily translated into a gain of capacity of the transport system, which is of special importance in railways which are already reaching their capacity limits. The wayside equipment would still be needed, for example, in cases where trains are in non-line of sight (NLOS). This would be the case in curved or single-track tunnels, or whenever they are far from each other. In these situations, the availability of a T2T link could hardly be guaranteed. However, in that case such a gain in transport capacity would not be necessary. In single track sections, trains can not directly communicate with those running in the opposite direction. Even so, the exchange of their MAs is of high importance with the preceding and upcoming trains, but not with those running in the opposite direction.

On the other hand, another interesting field in which T2T links could be used in railway communications is the transmission of video, especially of the closed circuit television (CCTV) images. The increasing quality of such systems sets a high demand in terms of capacity in the communication link. Therefore, the addition of this new link can be turned into a gain of capacity of the entire system with real-time video streaming. Whenever the quality of the T2G link of a train gets degraded, it could automatically switch the use to the T2T link and broadcast the images to the operations control center (OCC) via another train with a higher quality T2G link. It should also be remarked that this major upgrade in the CCTV system would be translated into safety improvements, both for passengers and the transport operator by enabling faster and more effective operations of the security staff.

Another functionality which yet remains as a future idea, is the virtual coupling concept for trains [3]. Similar to vehicle platooning in the automotive sector, virtual coupling is to be carried by radio T2T links between each consist [11,12]. Both consists would be connected through an ultra-reliable link to communicate braking and traction orders that would both be executed at the same time in every virtually coupled train. This would impact in a reduction of the distance between the trains, that could be smaller than the braking distance with no safety concerns as long as the reliability and availability of the link is ensured. Furthermore, a gain of capacity in the transport system could also be achieved, since only one train slot would be used by all the consists that form that virtual coupled train set (VCTS). This could be useful for freight trains among other scenarios.

As in CBTC, accurate positioning of each consist in a VCTS is essential. This can be achieved by absolute or relative measurements. In the first category, we would find the odometer system, for example, that obtains the position of each train together with the information that is periodically read from the balises to correct the errors. In the latter, we could find the use of extremely precise sensors that measure with a high degree of accuracy the distance with respect the preceding and posterior trains. Apart from the positioning, that does not actually imply the usage of a specific type of a communication link, this short distance between trains needs a low end to end delay, that could not be guaranteed by a T2G link.

3 Environment and Setup

Once the future applications for T2T in railway environments that have been exposed, the measurement campaign that this work presents is introduced. In these tests, the feasibility of a T2T link is analysed.

Fig. 2. Radio fixed at the windshield of the train [10].

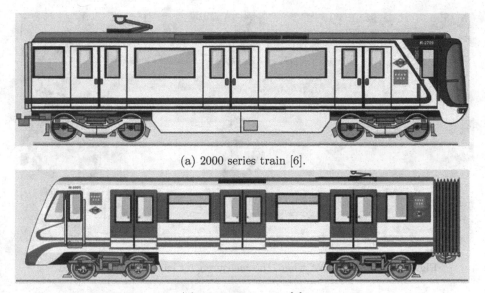

(a) 2000 series train [6].

(b) 3000 series train [6].

Fig. 3. Trains used for the measurement campaign.

For that purpose, two six-cars trains are used and one radio is placed at the windshield of each one as shown in Fig. 2. The radios have been gently supplied by Radwin.

3.1 Environment

Among the different series of trains that form the fleet of Metro de Madrid, trains of the 2000 and 3000 series each are selected, given that these are the ones that serve the Line 5, which connects to the depot where the campaign took place.

In Fig. 3a, the 2000 series train is depicted. Each car is 14.72 m long. Each composition is formed by 6 cars, yielding to a total length of 88.32 m, and can run up to 70 km/h. They were introduced between 1997 and 2005.

On the other hand, the 3000 series, shown in Fig. 3b, has a length of 89.38 m. In this case, it can reach up to 80 km/h, and were introduced between 2006 and 2008.

With respect to the scenario, the measurement took place in the Canillejas depot of Metro de Madrid. In two parallel test tracks, that can be seen in the bottom part of Fig. 4, the two mentioned trains are placed, one in each track. Both tracks are straight with an approximate length of 400 m.

Fig. 4. Canillejas depot where the measurement campaign was carried.

3.2 Setup

The model of radio used is TerraBridge [13], which is usually intended to connect different cars within the same consist, a situation where the antennas are almost always in line of sight (LOS). However, another mode of operation is selected for this work, which is aimed at connecting transmitters at distances of up to 250 m, ensuring a link establishment time smaller than 5 s. It operates at 60 GHz. The user can monitor the device in real time by accessing to the status of both the device and the link, the throughput or an activity log.

To test the link, the schemes in both trains, presented in Fig. 5, are exactly the same. Via a power over Ethernet (POE) device, a Raspberry Pi 3B+ is connected to the TerraBridge radio. The Raspberries are connected to some peripherals, such as a screen, a mouse, and a keyboard, that enable the control and configuration of the radios. Besides, its operative system offers interesting built-in tools such as ping, trace route or iperf3, which enable the testing of the performance of the link in real time. Some results are extracted in Sect. 4.

Apart from testing the link upon the radios with Radwin built-in functions of the native application, another functionality such as the video broadcast between the trains is tested. For that, a camera installed at the front of one of the trains transmits the images to the other. The selected model is the Axis P3905-R Mk II Network Camera, from Axis [1], a company whose products are mainly used in moving vehicles such as trains or buses. It delivers a high quality image of 1920×1080 of resolution and up to 30 frames per second (FPS).

In the train where the camera is installed, it is directly connected to the radio via Ethernet without the Raspberry, while in the other, the scheme remains unchanged. As for the Raspberries and the radios, the camera is assigned another IP address which is used in the receiving Raspberry to have access to the images through a real time streaming protocol (RTSP) connection.

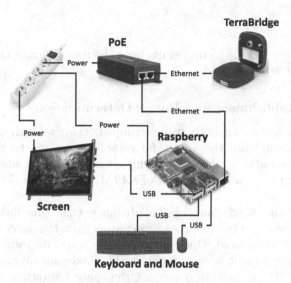

Fig. 5. Scheme of the setup for the measurements [10].

3.3 Tests

Finally, the different types of tests that were performed are introduced next. One of the goals of the campaign is to show that the link is stable enough even up to long distances. Besides, we would also want to check the compliance with the low time for link establishment.

For these purposes, a series of situations have been simulated:

- A train in front of the other, no movement.
- A train stopped and the other moving, both approaching and moving away.
- Two trains running at the same speed in the same direction (parallel running), separated by 10 m and 100 m

As outlined before, the performance of the link is to be tested with some of the built-in tools of the operative system. First we would find iperf3, an application that will generate UDP data flows, reporting each radio on the bandwidth and jitter periodically, per each sent packet. It follows a typical Client-Server architecture, and then, some of the parameters can only be obtained in one of the edges of the communication link. Moreover, with the typical ping application, the latency of a packet is obtained.

However, iperf3 and ping are applications of layer 4 and 3 respectively, which means that whenever a series of results are obtained, it should also be considered that they are given together with the processing times of each of the layers underneath. Then, the results must not be considered as a precise knowledge of the state of the physical channel but of its overall performance.

4   Results

In this section, the most relevant results from the measurement campaign in the Canillejas depot are presented.

4.1   Link Establishment and Range Determination

After an initial test, with both trains stopped, close to each other at a distance smaller than 10 m, the successful establishment of the communication link between the radios is checked. In this situation, the bandwidth used was 1.05 Mbps, transferring a total amount of 8.49 MB in 67 s. The delay was 0.05 ms with no packets lost.

Afterwards, the maximum possible distance that this link can cover is obtained as follows: one train starts moving away from the other while the state of the channel is monitored. Once the reception starts degrading at the point where packets are lost, it is considered as the maximum range of the system. However, it should be taken into account the space limitations of the scenario (recall that the length of the tracks is approximately 400 m). With that in mind, it was found that this range was 266.5 m.

4.2   Temporal Analysis

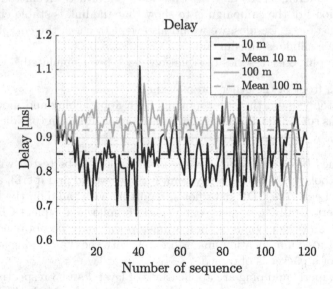

Fig. 6. Delay of the tests in the 2000 series train.

Interesting results are extracted in the situations where both trains run in parallel at the same speed of approximately 17 km/h. Two different distances, of 10 m and 100 m are tested.

In Fig. 6, the latency of the ping command is represented throughout the time, for both distances. Moreover, the average of this latency is also depicted. As expected, the average latency at 10 m of 0.85 ms is smaller than the one obtained at 100 m of 0.92 ms. However, in both situations, it is remarkably small.

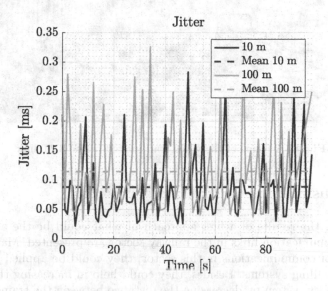

Fig. 7. Jitter of the tests in the 3000 series train.

Similar interpretations can be extracted from Fig. 7 where, thanks to the results obtained from the usage of the iperf3 tool, both the evolution of the jitter and its average value for each distance are represented. Again, the larger the distance is, the bigger the jitter becomes. In particular, the mean values for the jitter are 0.09 ms and 0.11 ms for 10 m and 100 m respectively, which is a small difference. Again, in absolute terms, the jitter times are very small as well in both cases. Finally, it should be highlighted the fact that the packet error rate (PER) or the total numbers of packets lost is 0 for both distances, denoting the high quality of the link in such situations.

4.3 Video Transmission

Finally, with the Axis camera, the video application over the wireless link between the TerraBridge radios is tested. In Fig. 8, a frame of the video broadcast in the receiving side is shown, with the receiving train highlighted in red. In all the situations that were tested (different distances, directions and speeds), the video quality is not perceived to suffer from any degradation. Then, it could be stated that a T2T communication link would be suitable so as to support the transmission of images in real time.

Fig. 8. A frame of the video transmitted in the T2T link.

5   Conclusions

In this work, the results of a first approach of what could be the applications for T2T communication links in the railway sector are presented. Mainly, as the current use of communications in this sector, they could be applied to increase safety in signalling systems. Besides, they could help in increasing the capacity of the transport system by decreasing the distance between the trains in CBTC systems with no safety penalty. This type of links could also help in increasing the capacity of the communications system itself to better accommodate high quality video images of the CCTV system among other services.

A measurement campaign in Metro de Madrid facilities is explained, involving two consists running in parallel tracks. The communication link is built upon two TerraBridge radios. With its built-in tools, the stability and reliability of the link is analysed. Besides, the video transmission captured from a CCTV camera is also tested. Then, it can be stated that the increase of the distance does not noticeably degrade the performance of the link, making these radios a good candidate for such an application.

As future work, apart from time figures, the rate could be increased in order to obtain the capacity of channel. On the other hand, effects of the misalignment of the antennas on the performance of the system could be considered with curved tracks. The effect of tunnels in the transmission could also be analysed. Besides, the effect of interfering trains should also be taken into consideration depending on the channel selection policy for each link. Moreover, we could go deeper and obtain much information about the physical channel itself while correlating that with the higher level results that are presented in this article. Finally, apart from the temporal resolution of the presented measurements, it would also be of interest to incorporate in the measurements a spatial resolution, both with a GPS or taking the data directly from the odometer system and the positioning balises of the track.

Acknowledgements. We would like to express our special thanks of gratitude to Radwin for having gently lent us two models of their TerraBridge radios.

We also thank Metro de Madrid for their kindness in making possible that the measurement campaign took place in their facilities, with two of their trains.

References

1. AXIS Communications. https://www.axis.com/es-es. Accessed 29 July 2021
2. Behaegel, R.: Sub 6 GHz MIMO channel sounder development based on software defined radio boards and LTE signal. Ph.D. thesis, Université de Lille (2021)
3. Bock, U., Varchmin, J.: Enhancement of the occupancy of railroads using virtually coupled train formations. In: World Congress on Railway Research (WCRR) (1999)
4. Briso-Rodríguez, C., Fratilescu, P., Xu, Y.: Path loss modeling for train-to-train communications in subway tunnels at 900/2400 MHZ. IEEE Antennas Wirel. Propag. Lett. **18**, 1164–1168 (2019)
5. Guan, K., et al.: Channel sounding and ray tracing for train-to-train communications at the THz band. In: 2019 13th European Conference on Antennas and Propagation (EuCAP), pp. 1–5 (2019)
6. treneando. todo sobre el mundo del tren. Todos los coches del metro de Madrid (y2). https://treneando.com/2016/05/02/todos-los-coches-del-metrode-madrid-y2/. Accessed 22 July 2021
7. Lehner, A., Garcia, C., Strang, T., Heirich, O.: Measurement and analysis of the direct train to train propagation channel in the 70 cm uhf-band. In: Nets4Cars/Nets4Trains (2011)
8. Lehner, A., Strang, T., Unterhuber, P.: Train-to-train propagation at 450 MHZ. In: 2017 11th European Conference on Antennas and Propagation (EUCAP), pp. 2875–2879 (2017)
9. Ma, S., Bu, B., Wáng, H.: A virtual coupling approach based on event-triggering control for CBTC systems under jamming attacks. In: 2020 IEEE 92nd Vehicular Technology Conference (VTC2020-Fall), pp. 1–6 (2020)
10. Mazuecos, B.: Diseño y prototipado de un sistema de señalización ferroviaria basada en comunicaciones directas entre vehículos (V2V). Master's thesis, Escuela Técnica Superior de Ingeniería de Telecomunicación, ETSIST, UPM, July 2021
11. Moreno, J., Riera, J., Haro, L., Rodríguez, C.: A survey on future railway radio communications services: challenges and opportunities. IEEE Commun. Mag. **53**, 62–68 (2015)
12. Parise, R., Dittus, H., Winter, J., Lehner, A.: Reasoning functional requirements for virtually coupled train sets: communication. IEEE Commun. Mag. **57**, 12–17 (2019)
13. RADWIN. https://www.radwin.com. Accessed 29 July 2021
14. Soliman, M., et al.: Dynamic train-to-train propagation measurements in the millimeter wave band - campaign and first results. In: 2019 13th European Conference on Antennas and Propagation (EuCAP), pp. 1–5 (2019)
15. Song, H., Schnieder, E.: Availability and performance analysis of train-to-train data communication system. IEEE Trans. Intell. Transp. Syst. **20**, 2786–2795 (2019)
16. Unterhuber, P., et al.: Wide band propagation in train-to-train scenarios - measurement campaign and first results. In: 2017 11th European Conference on Antennas and Propagation (EUCAP), pp. 3356–3360 (2017)

17. Wang, H., Zheng, W., Tian, Y.: The research on the performance enhancement with the application of v2v in CBTC systems. In: 2017 36th Chinese Control Conference (CCC), pp. 9998–10003 (2017)
18. Wang, X., Liu, L., Zhu, L., Tang, T.: Train-centric CBTC meets age of information in train-to-train communications. IEEE Trans. Intell. Transp. Syst. **21**(10), 4072–4085 (2020)
19. Yang, K., Berbineau, M., Ghys, J., Cocheril, Y., Seetharamdoo, D.: Propagation measurements with regional train at 60 GHZ for virtual coupling application. In: 2017 11th European Conference on Antennas and Propagation (EUCAP), pp. 126–130 (2017)
20. Zelenbaba, S., et al.: Characterization of time-variant wireless channels in railway communication scenarios. In: 2019 IEEE 2nd 5G World Forum (5GWF), pp. 536–541 (2019)

5G Technology for Next-Generation Wireless Consist Networks in Railways

Ana Larrañaga[1(✉)], Aitor Arriola[1], Imanol Martinez[1], Pedro Aljama[1],
Jérôme Härri[2], Igor Lopez[3], Uwe Fuhr[4], and Marvin Straub[4]

[1] Communication Systems, Ikerlan Technology Research Centre,
Arrasate/Mondragón, Spain
{ana.larranaga, aarriola, imartinez, paljama}@ikerlan.es

[2] Communication Systems, EURECOM, Sophia-Antipolis, France
haerri@eurecom.fr

[3] Technology Division, CAF R&D, Beasain, Spain
igor.lopez@caf.net

[4] IP-TCN Communication, Alstom, Mannheim, Germany
{uwe.fuhr, marvin.straub}@alstomgroup.com

Abstract. Currently, internal communications in trains are based on wired networks to provide Ultra-reliable Low Latency Communications (URLLC) for control and monitoring systems. However, these wired infrastructures are expensive to implement and maintain. Wireless Consist Networks (WLCN) can be a solution to this problem. Particularly, 5th Generation (5G) networks are considered one of the best options to support URLLC. This paper analyzes the use of 5G technology for a Wireless Consist Network (WLCN), as a replacement for the current wired network inside train consists. The goal of this analysis is to calculate which 5G configurations are capable of supporting the worst case of the required train backbone traffic. Obtained results indicate that 5G is a potential technology for sensor and end devices communication in the WLCN.

Keywords: 5G · Wireless · Consist · Railway

1 Introduction

CONNECTA-2 and Safe4RAIL-2 projects are researching on the use of wireless communications for the Next-Generation Train Control and Monitoring System (NG-TCMS). These projects belong to the Shift2Rail initiative of Horizon 2020, which aims at providing novel capabilities for railway industry through research and innovation, as stems out of its Multi Annual Action Plan [1].

The migration of the current wired Train Control and Monitoring System (TCMS) to a wireless architecture is one of the identified areas of opportunities that need to be tackled in the upcoming years. The TCMS is a communication bus that operates in a two-level network architecture: a Train Backbone (TB), which connects different consists or group of vehicles, and Consist Networks (CNs), which are individual networks located inside each consist. The NG-TCMS will apply wireless technologies at both backbone and consist levels, thus creating WireLess Train Backbone (WLTB)

J. Moreno García-Loygorri et al. (Eds.): Nets4Cars/Nets4Trains/Nets4Aircraft 2021, LNCS 13120, pp. 83–94, 2021.
https://doi.org/10.1007/978-3-030-92684-7_8

and WireLess Consist Network (WLCN) solutions, which will increase the flexibility, ease interoperability, and reduce the cost of the currently wired solution [2]. In a previous work a preliminary analysis was done for selecting wireless technologies to implement a WLCN [3]. This analysis concluded that no wireless technology currently available was capable of covering all NG-TCMS requirements for the WLCN. For that reason, the capabilities of 5G are explored in this work. A similar analysis was also done for the WLTB in a previous work [4].

The rest of the paper is organized as follows: Sect. 2 and Sect. 3 describe the railway and 5G networks. Section 4 and Sect. 5 explain the proposed wireless consists network architecture and the traffic requirements of end devices and sensors. Section 6 presents the analysis and the results of 5G technology for WLCN. Finally, Sect. 7 presents the conclusions of the presented work.

2   Railway Networking

In this section, we provide a brief introduction of Railway Networking concepts in order to better understand the innovative paradigms and challenges required by future wireless technologies.

2.1   Train Control and Monitoring System (TCMS)

The TCMS is a subsystem of railway vehicles which is required for the functional onboard integration. For integration of other subsystem (brakes, doors, etc.) the Train Communication Network (TCN) is used. The general TCN architecture is standardized (IEC 61375) as part of TCMS. This architecture defines a hierarchical structure with two levels of networks, Train Backbone (TBN) and Consist Network (CN), as depicted on Fig. 1.

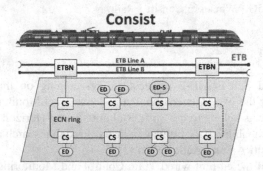

Fig. 1. Example of a simple train communication network (TCN) [3].

2.2   Ethernet Train Backbone (ETB)

Two technologies are covered by IEC 61375 series for Train Backbone: the Wire Train Bus (WTB) and the Ethernet Train Backbone (ETB). The WTB provides deterministic data delivery by performing cyclically with a period of 25 ms. It also allows sporadic data transmission for diagnostic uses. The content to be exchanged by WTB is specified by the UIC 556 standard. One of the main drawbacks found in WTB is its allowed data rate, which is limited to 1 Mbps as it makes use of RS-485 in the physical layer. The ETB is based on Ethernet and overcomes the data rate limitation of WTB with a physical layer able to support up to 100 Mbps. Equally to WTB, ETB allows dynamic train configuration in order to support train lengthening and shortening. The main shortcoming of ETB is that it is not deterministic, therefore not appropriate for time-sensitive functions.

A general problem which appears in both WTB and ETB is the installation and maintenance cost of Train Backbone. The reason for that is twofold. On the one hand the train backbone needs a dedicated wiring along the train which increases costs and becomes difficult to install in existing fleets. On the other hand, the connectors used between two trains when they are coupled are usually a source of failures due to the environmental conditions.

2.3 Ethernet Consist Network (ECN)

Consist Networks (CN) may be based on different technologies such as Multifunction Vehicle Bus (MVB), CANopen and Ethernet Consist Network (ECN) interfacing one Train Backbone. This paper is focused on ECN technology only. The ECN is an IP based network, interconnecting systems at car and consist levels. The ECN may use different topologies (ring or ladder structure) to achieve a robust and reliable communication network, distributing periodic and sporadic data. The network topology is built up by managed Consist Switches (CS). Other subsystems are connected to the switches to exchange information data within the consist and in the case of multiple consists also train wide (by making use of the ETB). A subsystem which is connected to the ECN is called end device (ED).

2.4 Wireless Railway Networking Challenges

One major innovation targeted for NG-TCMS is to replace wired parts of the railway vehicles by wireless technologies, with the objective to reduce cost, enhance maintenance and diagnosis as well as enable innovative applications such as wireless drive-by-wire or virtual coupling and train platoons. In this paper, we focus on the WLCN. Many challenges lie ahead, such as uncontrolled interferences, unreliable wireless links, unstable capacity and delay, not mentioning cyber-security.

3 5G Networks

5th Generation mobile network (5G) has been designed in order to support several vertical domains such as transport, health and manufacturing. 5G supports massive amounts of devices (Massive Machine Type Communication, mMTC), provides increased data rates (Enhanced Mobile Broadband, eMBB) and guarantees high reliability and low latency requirements (Ultra-Reliable and Low-Latency Communications,

URLLC). 5G has two fundamental parts which are the Radio Access Network (RAN) and the Core Network (CN). The UE (User Equipment) and the gNB (new generation Node B), the user and the base station respectively, are located within the RAN [5].

In 5G, a frame lasts 10 ms and it is composed of subframes with 1 ms duration (Fig. 2(a)). A subframe contains different number of slots. 5G supports different numerologies, which is the spacing between sub-carriers (SCS). The SCS goes from 15 kHz to 240 kHz, so the slot duration goes from 1 to 0.0625 ms. In addition, each slot has 14 symbols, except in the case of extended preamble which contains 12 symbols. The resource grid is characterized by one subframe in time domain and full carrier bandwidth in the frequency domain (Fig. 2(b)). There is one resource grid for each transmission direction (downlink (DL) or uplink (UL)), antenna port and sub-carrier spacing configuration. The carried bandwidth can be divided into Resource Blocks (RB). One RB has 12 subcarriers, whereas 1 subframe has 14 OFDM symbols × n° slots in a subframe OFDM symbols. A resource element (RE) is composed by one OFDM symbol in the time domain and one subcarrier in the frequency domain.

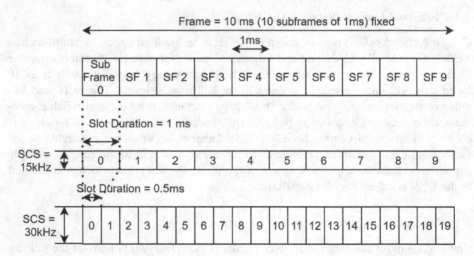

Fig. 2. 5G frame structure for SCS of 15 kHz and 30 kHz (a), and 5G resource grid for SCS of 15 kHz (b).

The resource elements can carry user data and control data. The DL control REs are Synchronization Signal Block (SSB), which is used for cell search, so the UEs acquires time and frequency synchronization with a cell and Channel Status Information (CSI) which is a mechanism used by the UEs to measure the quality of the radio channel and report the results to the gNB. Furthermore, Physical Downlink Shared Channel (PDSCH) is the physical channel that transmits user data in DL. The Demodulation Reference Signal (DM-RS) and Phase Tracking Reference Signal (PT-RS) are added to PDSCH. These two signals are reference signals and are generated within PDSCH. On the one hand, DM-RS is used to estimate the channel, on the other hand, PT-RS is used to compensate the Common Phase Error (CPE). For UL, Physical Random-Access Channel (PRACH), Sounding Reference Signal (SRS) and CSI are used as control signals. The PRACH is used by UEs to request an UL allocation from the base station, and it is the first message from UE to gNB. Moreover, Physical Uplink Shared Channel (PUSCH) transmits user data in UL as well as DMRS and PT-RS control signals.

In addition, 5G supports two operating bands [6]: Frequency Range 1 (FR1) frequencies below 7 GHz and Frequency Range 2 (FR2) that represents millimeter waves that are above 24 GHz. In FR1, the widest transmission bandwidth is 100 MHz with a full capacity of 273 RBs with a numerology (μ) of 1. In FR2, the widest transmission bandwidth is 400 MHz which uses 264 RBs with a μ of 3.

4 Proposed Wireless Consist Network Architecture

The WLCN covers the communications inside each consist and towards the WLTB. The main difference with the WLTB lies in the fact that the WLCN requires a higher number of nodes and has to operate in a more complex propagation environment (e.g. reflections on metallic structures and cabinets, influence of passengers, etc.). The Fig. 3 details the architecture proposed by CONNECTA-2 for the WLCN. This architecture is made of two redundant wireless networks, each of them having one Wireless Access Point (WAP) per vehicle. Wireless End Devices (WEDs) are connected to a WAP, except the Safe Wireless End Devices (WED-S), which will be connected to two WAPs for higher reliability, each one from a different wireless network, and therefore will require two wireless interfaces. On the other hand, all WAPs will be connected to Consist Switches (CS), which will be interconnected via a wired Ethernet Consist Network (ECN).

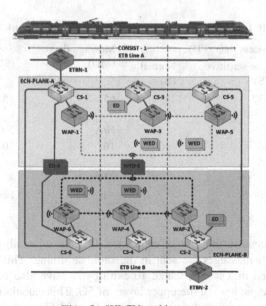

Fig. 3. WLCN architecture.

The previous approach is a suitable solution for the NG-TCN because it simplifies the integration of different wireless technologies, as in the case of 5G. For a 5G implementation, a WAP would be replaced by a gNB, and WEDs would be User Equipment-s (UEs). Figure 4 shows such a deployment, which follows a star topology where a gNB per car acts as a central node which manages the traffic flowing through the UEs. A maximum of 30 UEs are considered per car.

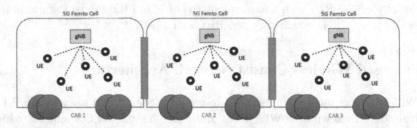

Fig. 4. Infrastructure-based 5G WLCN.

5 Wireless Consist Network (WLCN) Traffic

The requirements for the TCMS traffic of the Next-Generation Consist Network are detailed in Table 1, obtained from CONNECTA D3.1 Deliverable [7]. This traffic represents the typical consist TCMS traffic used in a wired network. The TCMS traffic includes three types of data: Process Data (PD) for small-sized and periodic data, Message Data (MD) which is bigger sized than PD and aperiodic data, and Supervisory Data (SD) which is periodic data used for supervision and for the inauguration process.

Table 1. TCMS Traffic requirements for consist network [7].

	Process data (PD)		Message data (MD)	Supervisory data (SD)
	Time sensitive (TS)	Normal (N)		
Data size (bytes)	1432	1432	65388	1500
Cycle time (ms)	1	1	N/A	50
Data rate (Mbps)	100	100	10	10
Latency (ms)	4	8	250	8
	Periodic		Aperiodic	Periodic

A worst-case scenario in terms of capacity will occur when all periodic (PD, SD) and aperiodic (MD) messages are sent in the same subframe. This worst-case calculation is summarized in Table 2, where 10 extra bytes have also been added to each traffic as an average payload of the upper layers of 5G. This calculation has been made for the traffic generated by end devices such as Central Control Units (CCUs); in a consist network there will be also additional devices such as sensors, who will have much lower traffic requirements. For sensors we can assume 100 bytes of Process Data every 1ms; with the addition of the extra bytes for the 5G upper layers, this will imply 880 bits per ms, which is much lower than the value required by end devices. This is also summarized in Table 2.

Table 2. Traffic generated per node (bits per ms).

	PD		MD	SD	Total
	TS	N			
End devices	11536	11536	10080	320	**33472**
Sensors	880	0	0	0	**880**

6 Analysis and Results of 5G Technology for WLCN

This section presents a numerical analysis of 5G capacity for a WLCN network. For this purpose, a customized resource-grid has been designed taking into account the control and user REs described in Sect. 3. This resource-grid design adopts the most restrictive configuration regarding the amount of resources occupied by reference signals. The configuration parameters are listed in Table 3.

Table 3. Resource grid: UL (left) and DL (right).

PRACH		**SSB**	
M (msg1-FSM)	8	Aggregation Level	16
SRS		Corest symbols	3
Symbols per slot	4	**CSI**	
Density per RB (kTC)	4	Density per RB	1
RBs	264	Slots density	4
CSI		**PDSCH**	
Density per RB	1	PT-RS RB density	2
Slots density	4	PT-RS time density	1
PUSCH		DMRS time type	A
PT-RS RB density	2	DMRS length	1
PT-RS time density	1	Additional DMRS symbols	0
DMRS time type	A	DMRS freq type	2
DMRS length	2	DMRS freq density	4
Additional DMRS symbols	0		
DMRS freq type	2		
DMRS freq density	4		

Considering the designed resource grid in Table 3, Table 4 indicates the maximum capacity that FR1 and FR2 bands are able to provide for different antenna configurations and Modulation Coding Scheme (MCS) values. To obtain the most restrictive scenario, it is assumed that the periodic and aperiodic data, as well as the control and user data are transmitted in the same subframe. As it is a control and monitoring system deployment, a symmetrical bandwidth division is assumed for UL and DL transmissions. It is further considered that the streams of codeword encodings are mapped directly to RF ports and physical antennas, enabling spatial multiplexing. First, the total number of REs inside a subframe are calculated (Eq. 1):

Table 4. Maximum 5G capacity (Mbps).

		Antennas	MCS index			
			0	10	20	28
Up	FR1	1	6	33	83	138
		2	12	66	166	277
		3	18	99	248	415
		4	23	132	331	554
	FR2	1	36	205	512	856
		2	72	409	1024	1711
		3	108	614	1535	2567
		4	144	818	2047	3423
Down	FR1	1	9	49	112	205
		2	18	97	223	409
		3	27	146	335	614
		4	35	194	446	818
	FR2	1	38	207	474	869
		2	75	413	948	1738
		3	113	620	1422	2608
		4	150	826	1896	3477

$$TotalRE_{persubframe} = RB_{intheBW} \times 2^{\mu} \times 14\,sym \times 12\,subcarriers \qquad (1)$$

Therefore, the $TotalRE_{persubframe}$, with numerology (μ) 1, is 273 RBs $\times 2^1 \times 14$ symbols $\times$ 12 subcarriers which is equal to 91728 REs and $TotalRE_{persubframe}$, with numerology 3, is 264 RBs $\times 2^3 \times 14$ symbols $\times$ 12 subcarriers which is equal to 354816 RE-s. Then, considering the antenna layers and removing the REs that are used for signalling (Table 3) from the $TotalRE_{persubframe}$, the number of REs for DL or UL that are used for data transmission are obtained (Eq. 2):

$$RE_{PUSCH/PDSCH} = antennaLayers \times \left(\frac{TotalRE_{persubframe}}{2} - RefSignal_{UL/DL} \right) \quad (2)$$

Finally, the maximum 5G capacity is calculated using equation (Eq. 3). To calculate these values, the REs per PUSCH/PDSCH, UL and DL respectively and the MCS of 0, 10, 20 and 28 values [8, table 5.1.3.1-1] are used.

$$Capacity(Mbps)_{max} = \frac{RE_{PUSCH/PDSCH} \times codingRate \times ModulationOrder}{10^6} \times 1000$$

$$(3)$$

Required 5G bit rates can be obtained (Eq. 4) for different MCS configurations and for an increasing number of nodes applying the traffic detailed in Table 2 (Eq. 4, $totalBits_{1ms}$) to this resource-grid. Up to 30 nodes have been considered in this analysis, which is the maximum number of devices per car/femtocell.

$$Capacity(Mbps)_{n^{\circ}Nodes} = n^{\circ}Nodes \times \frac{totalBits_{1ms}}{codingRate \times ModulationOrder} \times \frac{1000}{10^6} \quad (4)$$

The results obtained are shown in Fig. 5 (UL) and Fig. 6 (DL) for end devices, and in Fig. 7 for sensors (only UL has been considered for sensors). The results presented are for an MCS value of 28. These figures compare the capacity needed by end devices and sensors to transmit in 1ms the traffic pattern chosen in Table 2 versus the actual capacity that 5G can support depending on different configurations (Table 4). As can be seen in Fig. 5 and Fig. 6, the maximum capacity supported by DL is higher than the maximum capacity supported by UL. This is due to the fact that UL needs more resources to transmit control signals than DL (Table 3). Apart from that, an MCS 28 configuration is able to handle correctly all the traffic required by 30 sensors (Fig. 7), while in the case of end devices, for UL (Fig. 5), 5G with FR1 and 1 antenna is not able to transmit the chosen data having 25 or more nodes.

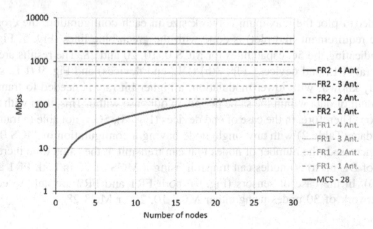

Fig. 5. Required traffic vs 5G capacity (UL) – MCS 28 (end devices) (Color figure online)

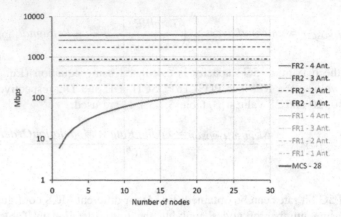

Fig. 6. Required traffic vs 5G capacity (DL) – MCS 28 (end devices) (Color figure online)

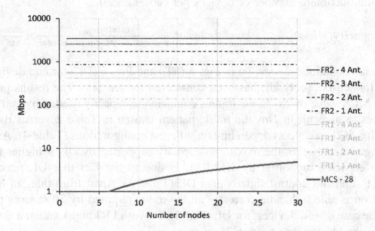

Fig. 7. Required traffic vs 5G capacity (UL) – MCS 28 (sensors) (Color figure online)

In order to plot the maximum network size in each configuration, the crossing of the traffic requirement (red plot) is done with the green/blue lines (Fig. 5, Fig. 6 and Fig. 7) indicating the 5G capabilities for MCS 0, 10, 20 and 28. The results are plotted in Fig. 8 (a) (UL, end devices), Fig. 8(b) (DL, end devices) and Fig. 9 (UL, sensors). As already known, with lower modulation, a higher bit rate is needed to transmit the same amount of data within the same period, in our case within 1ms, than with a higher modulation. Therefore, in the case of end devices (Fig. 8), 5G is not able to transmit the required data (Table 2) with any single node having a configuration of MCS 0. As the MCS is increased, the number of nodes that can transmit at the same time increases, in the case of DL up to 30 nodes can transmit using a MCS of 28 in both FR1 and FR2 (Fig. 8(b)). In the case of sensors (Fig. 9), both FR1 and FR2 are able to cover the whole network of 30 nodes using either MCS 10, 20 or MCS 28.

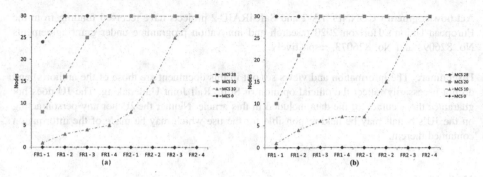

Fig. 8. Maximum network size (a) UL and (b) DL – end devices

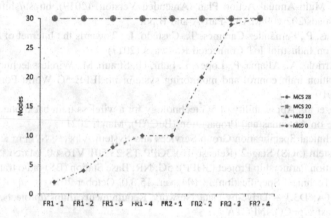

Fig. 9. Maximum network size UL – sensors

7   Conclusions

In this paper an analysis has been done about the usage of 5G technology as a replacement for the current wired network inside train consists. For this purpose, the required traffic values have been obtained both for end devices and sensors, and this traffic has been mapped against the capabilities offered by different configurations of 5G. Obtained results indicate that 5G is a potential technology for sensor and end devices communication in the WLCN, even though specific MCS configurations should be selected for maximum node coverage in worst-case traffic scenarios.

Finally, it should be noted that the analysis presented in this paper has been focused on TCMS traffic, but train devices also generate On-Board and Multimedia Services (OMTS) traffic, which includes streaming audio, video and best effort data. This traffic has more relaxed time requirements than TCMS, and therefore could be covered by a separate wireless system with different capabilities.

Acknowledgment. CONNECTA-2 and Safe4RAIL-2 projects have received funding from the European Union's Horizon 2020 research and innovation programme under grant agreements No. 826098 and No. 826073, respectively.

Disclaimer. The information and views set out in this document are those of the author(s) and do not necessarily reflect the official opinion of Shift2Rail Joint Undertaking. The JU does not guarantee the accuracy of the data included in this article. Neither the JU nor any person acting on the JU's behalf may be held responsible for the use which may be made of the information contained therein.

References

1. Shift2Rail: Multi-Annual Action Plan (Amended Version) (2019). https://shift2rail.org/wp-content/uploads/2020/09/MAAP-Part-A-and-B.pdf
2. Fraga-Lamas, P., Fernández-Caramés, T., Castedo, L.: Towards the Internet of Smart Trains: A Review on Industrial IoT-Connected Railways (2017)
3. Härri, J., Arriola, A., Aljama, P., Lopez, I., Fuhr, U., Straub, M.: Wireless technologies for the next-generation train control and monitoring system. In: IEEE 5G World Forum, Dresden, October 2019
4. Aljama, P., et al.: Applicability of 5G technology for a wireless train backbone. In: European Conference on Antennas and Propagation (EuCAP), March 2021
5. 3GPP: Technical Specification Group Services and System Aspects; System architecture for the 5G System (5GS) Stage2 (Release 16) 3GPP TS 23.501 V16.4.0, March 2020
6. 3rd Generation Partnership Project (3GPP): 5G; NR; Base Station (BS) radio transmission and reception, Technical Specification 38.104, ver. 15.3.0, October 2018
7. CONNECTA: D3.1 – Drive-by-Data Network Requirements. https://projects.shift2rail.org/s2r_ip1_n.aspx?p=CONNECTA
8. 3GPP: 5G;NR; Physical layer procedures for data. Technical Specification 38.214 version 16.2.0 Release 16 (2020)

Author Index

Printed in the United States
by Baker & Taylor Publisher Services